Cultures in Conflict

Cultures in Conflict

Eliminating Racial Profiling

Second Edition

Martha R. Bireda

ROWMAN & LITTLEFIELD EDUCATION

A division of

ROWMAN & LITTLEFIELD PUBLISHERS, INC.
Lanham • New York • Toronto • Plymouth, UK

Published by Rowman & Littlefield Education
A division of Rowman & Littlefield Publishers, Inc.
A wholly owned subsidiary of The Rowman & Littlefield Publishing Group, Inc.
4501 Forbes Boulevard, Suite 200, Lanham, Maryland 20706
http://www.rowmaneducation.com

Estover Road
Plymouth PL6 7PY
United Kingdom

British Library Cataloguing in Publication Information Available

Library of Congress Cataloging-in-Publication Data

Bireda, Martha R.
    Cultures in conflict : eliminating racial profiling / Martha R. Bireda.—2nd ed.
        p. cm.
    Rev. ed. of: Eliminating racial profiling in school discipline. Includes bibliographical references.
    ISBN 978-1-60709-337-4 (cloth : alk. paper)—ISBN 978-1-60709-338-1 (pbk. : alk. paper)—ISBN 978-1-60709-339-8 (electronic)
    1. School discipline—United States.   2. Discrimination in education—United States.
    I. Bireda, Martha R. Eliminating racial profiling in school discipline.   II.   Title.
    LB3012.2.B57 2010
    371.5089—dc22   2009031908

Printed in the United States of America

♾ ™ The paper used in this publication meets the minimum requirements of American National Standard for Information Sciences—Permanence of Paper for Printed Library Materials, ANSI/NISO Z39.48-1992.

*Dedicated to African American male students,
who, because they are feared and misunderstood,
are denied equal educational opportunity.*

Contents

PART III

Foreword

It is an honor to write the foreword for the latest edition of *Cultures in Conflict: Eliminating Racial Profiling in Schools* by Dr. Martha Bireda. The disciplining of students remains an area in education that is not adequately addressed, particularly the disciplining of African American males. In fact, student discipline is a symptom of a much greater problem in schools, one that is connected to a student's self worth, level of motivation, and ultimate success in school.

Educators can't change a student's family background or the fact that they live in impoverished circumstances, but they do have the power to transform what happens in a school setting. This includes providing students with a rich curriculum and effective instruction where high expectations are the norm, and creating a positive and supportive school environment where children are valued and are held responsible for their actions.

The school discipline numbers from across the country reveal that African American males are frequently the ones caught in the discipline bind. They are often stereotyped and pushed into bad behavior. There are also cultural and gender differences at play that reflect the sky-high discipline rates for African American males.

This is not to say that teachers are entirely at fault. Today's educators are under a great deal of pressure with everything from high-stakes testing and demanding parents to a loaded curriculum. But many come to the profession with unconscious conditioned cultural beliefs. Educators should be encouraged to engage in critical reflection about their own beliefs and attitudes concerning every child's capacity to learn and be successful. Ultimately a change in school discipline begins with the school administrators and requires a shift in attitude. It also requires that parents be involved in the process.

Dr. Bireda, a counselor by profession, makes a compelling argument in this book about the current issues associated with student discipline, their sources, and how to create a culturally sensitive school. She includes ethical questions for educators to respond to, approaches for ensuring discipline events don't escalate, and guidelines for action. It is my hope that every educator in America takes Dr. Bireda's critical message into their schools (and classrooms) and acts on it.

Paula Egelson, Ed.D.
Director, Center for Partnerships to Improve Education
College of Charleston
Charleston, South Carolina

Acknowledgments

A very special thanks to

Dr. Tom Koerner, who many years ago first encouraged me to write about equity in education.

Dr. Russell Skiba, whose years of excellent research related to racial disparity in discipline was invaluable in writing this book.

Dr. Nancy Peck, for encouraging me to write about the racial disparity in school discipline. Dr. Peck's dedicated work in the equity field for more than thirty years has been an inspiration to me.

Dawn Spivey, who through our many talks on travels to school districts became my "muse."

Dr. J. Vann Sikes, Mr. Jay Brinson, and the talented members of the Superintendent's Advisory Committee in Crisp County, Georgia, for permission to use their excellent materials in this publication.

The Atlanta Office of Civil Rights, for generously providing discipline statistics.

Julia Potter of WEEA, for her suggestions and encouragement.

To the parent group and their advisor, Dr. Betty Dunlap, from Harris County Georgia.

Dr. Paula Egelson, director of the Center for Partnerships in Education at the College of Charleston for providing me the opportunity to again observe and work with students.

The year spent as a visiting professor has provided new insights that are included in the new edition.

Charlene Sanabria, who worked tirelessly to arrange opportunities for me to talk to and work with students.

Alverta Bowens, whose caring and commitment to students makes me ever mindful of the importance of this work.

Maera Stratton for her guidance and thoughtful feedback about the manuscript.

The many students and parents who over the years have shared their stories, and enabled me to have real insight into the problem of racial disparity in school discipline.

Introduction

The first edition of *Cultures In Conflict* (2002) had its genesis almost 20 years ago, when an African American principal requested that I visit his middle school in a small, Southern school district. He was concerned that he and his office were being inundated with discipline referrals for African American students, especially males.

The principal showed me files filled with referrals, most of which he felt were unwarranted. I spent three days at the school, talking to parents, teachers, and students. My plan was to conduct a workshop for teachers after gathering information from the three groups. The students who were sent to me (not specifically at my request) turned out to be the "problem" students.

It was early in the second semester of school, and some of the students in the group had received as many as fifty-plus referrals to the principal's office. The students whom I talked to that day and the students who had been described to me by teachers appeared to be two entirely different groups. I talked to a group of students who honestly and openly admitted that they misbehaved, but also expressed a great deal of anger and pain.

There was one young man, however, a tall, rather heavyset youngster who appeared to be older than his actual age, who touched me deeply. In fact, I will never forget the sadness in his eyes and the pain in his voice when he responded to my inquiry as to why he had so many referrals. With a great deal of respect to me, he said, "Ma'am, if you were in my shoes for one day, how would you react?" That day, I started to really listen to students, especially the "bad kids," and to hear their experiences and their pain.

After that experience, I designed a workshop for administrators and teachers to help reduce the number of disciplinary referrals for African

American students, especially males. It was not until 2000, almost ten years later, that everything I felt as an educator, counselor, and equity consultant was affirmed.

Three national studies confirmed that there is more to the racial disparity in discipline than meets the eye. These studies provided the data that left no doubt that we as teachers and administrators must look more closely at the school climate, teacher–student relationships, and the in-school experiences of African American students if we are to drastically reduce the disproportionate numbers of disciplinary referrals and sanctions for African American students.

As I write this updated edition, I am both dismayed and saddened by the lack of progress that has been made since the first edition was published. At that time, racial disparity in discipline was considered a "civil rights" issue, and the Office of Civil Rights vigorously investigated parental complaints and claims of discrimination in disciplinary policies and practices. In the past decade, there has seemingly been a retreat from the pursuit of educational equity as it relates to discipline.

In 2009, racial disparity in discipline remains a critical and unresolved issue in education. In fact, the problem has gotten worse instead of better. The frequency of out-of-school suspension and expulsion is increasing (Rausch and Skiba, 2009), with a near doubling of the number of students suspended annually since 1974 (Wald and Losen, 2003).

Zero tolerance policies and the pressures of high stakes testing have exacerbated the problem, and "exclusionary discipline" has become the norm. The problem is just as severe and perhaps even more severe in schools serving predominately minority populations.

The changing demographics of the national school population and especially "the browning of America" has made it necessary to view racial disparity in discipline in the larger sociopolitical context of education in this country, which includes the disparate treatment of students termed by John Ogbu (1978) as caste or involuntary minorities.

Ogbu describes caste or involuntary minorities as groups that have been enslaved, conquered, or colonized, and have been considered biologically, intellectually, and culturally inferior. These groups historically, have been excluded and stigmatized by the larger mainstream society. Students from these groups, i.e., African Americans, Mexican Americans, Puerto Rican Americans, Native Americans, and Pacific Islanders, have and do still suffer disparate treatment in our schools.

It is students from caste/involuntary minority groups who are disproportionately represented among those referred, suspended, and expelled from school. In some school districts in the Northwest, where they are highly represented in the school population, students from the Pacific Islands (colonized) have the highest expulsion and suspension rates of any ethnic or racial groups.

In other school districts, disproportionate numbers of Native American students are suspended and expelled from school. Among the caste/involuntary minorities in our schools, African American and Hispanic/Latino students (the largest groups represented) are most often disproportionately disciplined. African American students, however, especially African American males, receive the most harsh and unfair discipline.

The primary focus of the updated edition of this book will continue to be African American students, especially males, because they are the group that continues to be most disproportionately represented in disciplinary referrals, suspensions, and expulsions. The information and strategies suggested in this book can however, be adapted and applied in any school setting in which the culture of any group of students is misunderstood and where culturally conditioned beliefs are held which impact their relationships with teachers and administrators.

This book is especially designed to provide administrators and teachers with knowledge of behaviors and precipitating factors that increase the potential for African American students, especially male students, to be referred for disciplinary actions. Specifically, the reader will gain an awareness of the culturally influenced communication style of African American male students that often contributes to tension in classroom interactions with their teachers.

In addition, the reader will become aware of the culturally conditioned beliefs and assumptions about African American students, especially males that affect teacher–student rapport and relationships. Finally, this book provides teachers and administrators with a set of strategies that can be utilized to reduce the high frequency of disciplinary referrals and actions involving African American students.

A majority of teachers are white and female; this book can be of particular assistance in helping them to better understand the culturally based and culturally conditioned factors that influence disciplinary incidents involving African American male students. This book will also be beneficial to African American and other teachers who may desire to better understand how the social class of the teacher and student has an influence on the student–teacher interaction and disciplinary incidents.

The 2009 edition has been expanded to include two new chapters. In part 1, examine system-related factors that contribute to the racial disparities in discipline are examined. In Chapter 1, an overview of current research data related to racial disproportionality in discipline is presented; Chapter 2 deals with the impact of No Child Left Behind and high stakes testing upon racial disparity in discipline; in Chapter 3, *school-related* factors that are the by-products of institutional racism and that place African American students, especially males, at risk for disciplinary actions are discussed.

Part 2 addresses the influence of culturally based and culturally conditioned factors on classroom interactions between the African American student and his teachers. Chapter 4 deals with the impact of the African American and Hispanic/Latino student's culture; Chapter 5 addresses communication differences that can be problematic in the classroom; Chapter 6 explores the impact of conscious and unconscious stereotyping of the African American male in particular; and Chapter 7 describes how cultural conflicts and stereo-typing lead to inequities in the classroom.

In part 3, strategies for creating culturally responsive and accepting school environments for African American students, as well as for eliminating disparities in discipline referrals and sanctions, are provided. In Chapter 8, the school culture and climate are examined; specific strategies are given for the administrator's role in changing the school climate (Chapter 9) ; changing individual attitudes (Chapter 10); working with parents and the community (Chapter 11); and evaluating the change process (Chapter 12) are discussed.

The material included in this new expanded edition is the result of a year spent observing in classrooms, talking to teachers, and listening to students who attended "underachieving" predominately African American schools in a Southeastern state. Issues brought to the forefront during the past decade have created the necessity to address the following in the new edition: (1) the relationship between the discipline gap and the achievement gap; (2) the ways in which authoritarian, punitive, and controlling school climates contribute to disciplinary events.

The ultimate goal of this book is to assist teachers and administrators in reducing disciplinary events that contribute to the decreased academic performance of students whose race and culture impacts their experiences in the school setting and contributes to their over-representation among those referred, suspended, and expelled. Any student who is idle while sitting in the office, assigned to in-school suspension, out-of-school without the benefit of instruction, or placed in inadequate alternative educational settings cannot and will not experience academic success.

As we enter the twenty-first century, it is urgent that we as educators reach out to all students, and find ways to ensure that they have positive, successful experiences, and remain in school until graduation. A significant step in this direction is finally and resolutely addressing the long-standing problem of racial disparity in discipline.

Workshops

Dr. Bireda presents keynote addresses and conducts workshops for administrators, teachers, and parents related to disparity in discipline and the achievement gap.

If you would like to receive information about keynote addresses or workshops, please contact

The Bireda Group
P.O. Box 510818
Punta Gorda, Florida 33951
(239) 823-2911
biredagrp@aol.com

Part I

Chapter 1

Discipline

The New Equity Issue

The mechanisms employed to deny equal educational opportunity to caste/involuntary minority students have taken many forms, from de facto segregation to inadequate funding to academic tracking. Today, disproportional, extreme, and unwarranted discipline is a major means by which students from caste/involuntary minority groups are deprived of educational equity. Whether deliberate or unintentional, African American and Hispanic/Latino students, particularly males, are trapped in a vicious cycle that leads to dropping out, and being a victim of the "school-to-prison pipeline."

Racial disparity in discipline first received national attention when the Children's Defense Fund (1975) reported that Black students were two to three times more likely to be suspended than Whites, received lengthier suspensions, were more likely to be repeatedly suspended, and were suspended at younger ages.

At the time, it appeared that this phenomenon was merely a symptom of the "growing pains" associated with desegregation efforts. The "burden of fitting in" in desegregated schools was placed largely on Black students.

Eyler et al. (1983) reported that newly desegregated districts suspended and expelled disproportionate numbers of Black students, and Black students were more likely to be suspended for "subjective" or "discretionary" offenses, (i.e., disobedience, disruptive or disrespectful behaviors).

A PERSISTENT PROBLEM

Almost thirty years after U.S. schools were generally considered to be fully desegregated, racial disparity in discipline continued to be a significant problem. The magnitude of the problem was evidenced by two national studies.

Researchers from the Advancement Project and the Civil Rights Project at Harvard (2000) found that Black and Latino students were more likely to be referred for disciplinary actions, to be disciplined for minor conduct, to receive punishments disproportionate to their conduct, and to be referred for "discretionary" offenses.

The researchers also revealed what would become a disturbing and persistent trend for years to come:

- Out-of-school suspensions for Black students were disproportionate to their representation in the school enrollment nationally; Black students represented 17 percent of national enrollment, but 32 percent of out-of-school suspensions.
- Black males were disciplined more often and more severely than any other minority group.

Skiba et al. (2002, p. 338) examined a number of alternatives to explain gender, race, and socioeconomic disproportionality, none of which were capable of accounting for the disparities between black and white students. They concluded that "to the extent that these alternative hypothesis can be ruled out, it becomes more likely that highly consistent statistical discrepancies in school punishment for black and white students are an indicator of systematic and prevalent bias in the practice of school discipline."

More recent studies indicate that racial disparity in discipline remains a serious problem in school districts across the nation. Wallace et al. (2008) studied large national samples of White, Black, Hispanic, Asian American, and American Indian students to examine patterns and trends in racial, ethnic, and gender differences in school discipline.

They found that Black, Hispanic, and American Indian youth were slightly more likely to be sent to the office and substantially (two to five times) more likely to be suspended or expelled. Most significantly, they found that although school discipline rates decreased over time for most ethnic groups, among Black students, school discipline rates increased between 1991 and 2005.

U.S. Department of Education data for the 2004–2005 school year, analyzed by the Chicago Tribune (2007), revealed racial inequality in suspensions and expulsions nationwide. The report indicated that

- In every state except Idaho, Black students were being suspended in numbers greater than would be expected from their proportion of the school population.

- In 21 states, the disproportionality was so pronounced that the percentage of Black suspensions was more than double their percentage of the student body.
- On average, across the nation, Black students were suspended and expelled at nearly three times the rate of White students. No other ethnic group was disciplined at such a high rate.

As was found in earlier studies, this research indicated that

- Black students were no more likely to misbehave than other students from the same social and economic environments.
- Poverty alone could not explain the disparities.
- When measured in terms of disciplinary sanctions, such as suspensions and expulsions, schools in the U.S. remained unequal.

The most disturbing aspect of the report was that "only about six percent" of school districts across the nation acknowledged the issue of racial disparity in discipline and made efforts to address the problem. As this book goes to press, there is no sign that the problem of racial disparity in discipline is abating.

ZERO TOLERANCE

The 1990s ushered in the era of zero tolerance or "get tough" discipline in schools. Zero tolerance became national policy with the Gun-Free Schools Act of 1994. While the law initially pertained to and mandated expulsion for possession of a firearm, school districts across the country broadened the law to cover a range of subjectively defined behaviors such as disrespect, disobedience, and disorderly conduct (Skiba and Knestry, 2001; Browne et al., 2001).

While the application of zero-tolerance policies was intended to be "color-blind" and to mete out equally harsh punishment, the expansion of the mandate has disproportionately impacted caste/involuntary minorities. In light of the historical treatment of students from caste minorities in our schools, it is not surprising that they unfairly bear the overwhelming brunt of zero-tolerance policies. In fact, zero-tolerance policies are more likely to exist in predominately Black and Latino school districts (The Advancement Project and the Civil Rights Project at Harvard University, 2000).

THE PRICE OF DISPARITY IN DISCIPLINE

For over thirty years, we have documented a major equity problem related to discipline in our schools. By now, at least a generation of children, like the young man that I encountered, has cried out but we as educators have failed to hear them. Instead of looking at ourselves and the school environment, we have concluded that single-parent homes, the lack of role models, television, and rap music are the sole reasons for the enormous discipline gap in our schools today.

When students perceive inconsistencies in rules, detect favoritism, or feel disrespected and ostracized, they become angry, lose respect for us as adults, create ways to protect themselves emotionally, strike back, and become alienated from the learning process. Meirer et al. (1989) suggests that any type of discrimination, be it in academic grouping or disciplinary procedures, has predictable results; students become disillusioned and drop out or are pushed out (in the case of suspensions and expulsions), or they do graduate but do not receive the same quality of education as other students receive.

Racial disparity in discipline is a symptom of a deeper problem that schools must face. It is not an easy issue to address and requires a deeper commitment than designing programs to change student behavior. This book is intended to address the root causes of racial disparity in discipline and to provide school districts and educators with a "road map" for those who choose to make the commitment.

No Child Left Behind and the high stakes testing movement has had a tremendous impact on the educational experiences of students from caste/involuntary minority groups. In Chapter 2, we will examine the impact of NCLB policies and practices upon the already serious problem of racial disparity in discipline.

RECOMMENDATIONS

Do: Review your school's discipline statistics.

- Ask: Who gets suspended? For what type of offenses?
- What does this data reflect?

Chapter 2

A New Urgency

No Child Left Behind and the high stakes testing movement have created a new urgency to examine the issue of racial disparity in discipline. While ostensibly designed to increase the achievement of caste/involuntary minorities and to close the racial achievement gap, the policies and practices engendered by NCLB are in fact breeding more failure among the most vulnerable groups. NCLB has only exacerbated the already serious problem of racial disparity in discipline.

The stress imposed by NCLB has increased teacher intolerance for the behaviors of students whose culture is misunderstood and whose image is already tarnished by stereotyping. Students perceived to be troublesome take away from mandated instructional time and lower test scores. One teacher described the attitudes of his colleagues following a meeting to decrease the number of students being referred as the semester was drawing to a close, "as wanting to be rid of their nuisances for the rest of the year."

The requirements for academic achievement and yearly progress have also heightened the pressure for administrators to remove "troublesome" students. The exit of these students creates the appearance of rising test scores, thus increasing the school's ratings. Zero tolerance provides the means to exclude these students.

NCLB has also created a climate for increased disciplinary events among students from caste/involuntary minority groups who subsequently become the recipients of exclusionary discipline. Some factors that influence an increase in disciplinary events are (1) the type and pace of instruction and (2) the general classroom climate (the school climate will be addressed in Chapter 8.

TYPE AND PACE OF INSTRUCTION

"Drill and kill joy" instruction which focuses on "everything that might be on the test" leads to student boredom, frustration, and misbehavior. Students complain about the ubiquitous worksheet and "everyday, the same old thing." Often the only excitement that students experience in class is when a student misbehaves.

The pace at which content must be covered is also problematic; when instructional time is allocated by the clock, there is little time to provide help "in the moment." While students can often receive afterschool tutoring, questions go unanswered, material is not fully understood, and "time sensitive" explanations of content are lacking.

With NCLB, culturally responsive instruction has been abandoned as "teaching to the test" has become the norm. There is a general disregard for cultural learning styles or instructional approaches that would best suit students from diverse cultures. All of this makes for students whose instructional needs are not met, who become bored, alienated, disengaged from the learning process, and who in turn misbehave in class.

• CLASSROOM CLIMATE: NCLB has produced classroom environments that are rigid and controlled. There is no place for humor or fun. Many young students are now denied time to release excess energy as recess periods have been lessened or totally eliminated in some elementary schools. This sets up boys, especially African American boys who tend to be very energetic for disciplinary problems.

As teachers are fearful of students, especially African American males, and of losing control of the classroom, classroom activities are highly structured and monotonous. The type of cooperative learning and group problem solving that most motivates African American students is taboo. Students complain that "they are afraid to let us work in groups because they think they will lose control." Again with no outlet for creative or just adolescent energy, disciplinary events are bound to occur.

The Academic/Discipline Cycle of Failure

While observing in "underachieving" predominately African American schools, I noted a pattern which I termed the *academic/discipline cycle of failure* that is played out daily in classrooms. Most often the discipline event involves a low achieving student and one who may have previously been suspended. Some students have perfected this process to the "art of escape."

The process that occurs as the discipline event is precipitated, developed, and progressed is described below:

Precipitating Event

• An activity is initiated or introduced that will require student performance. The student becomes overwhelmed by a fear of public exposure or ridicule and desires to escape the situation. For instance, being called upon to go to the blackboard in Math class can initiate an event.

Initiation of Disciplinary Event

• The student employs a typical ruse or escape tactic, e.g., beginning a conversation with another student, starting to clown around, getting up and walking around, claiming to have no pencil or paper, or simply refusing to work.

Progression of the Disciplinary Event

• The teacher moves immediately to quell the disturbance. His/her desire is to prevent a disruption which will result in the loss of instructional time or perceived loss of control. He or she may not understand the student's motivation or be aware of the pattern.
• The teacher writes a referral for the student to be removed from class.

Consequences of the Disciplinary Event

• The student is sent to ISS for the class period. He or she escapes the uncomfortable situation and experiences a sense of temporary relief.
• The student fails to get the benefit of instruction for that period or any class work (the teacher may or may not send work to ISS for the student depending upon his/her attitude toward the student).
• The student returns to class the next day unprepared, further behind, more frustrated and fearful.
• The cycle repeats.

There is the possibility that the next discipline event involving this student will escalate when the student returns to class. Even though the student was able to escape the discomfort of the previous situation, he knows that he is now further behind. He is even more fearful and determined to avoid discomfort and embarrassment. This progression of the disciplinary event often occurs in this way:

- Student raises hand to say that he does not understand. He is either ignored or told that it is his fault that he missed the material.
- The student feels embarrassed now as well as frustrated. He ups the ante by making some remark to his classmates or the teacher.
- The teacher responds with sarcasm or some belittling remark.
- The student feels embarrassed, angry, and perceives that the teacher "does not care." The student may use profanity or become disrespectful at this point.
- The teacher writes a referral.
- The student this time more likely will receive an OSS for disrespect of the teacher and disruption of the class.
- The student escapes both a humiliating and frustrating situation but falls much farther behind.
- With each discipline event, and subsequent suspension, the student's chances of catching up and performing adequately in class are diminished. This pattern will likely continue unless some intervention occurs.

The academic/discipline cycle of failure is the natural result of students missing instructional time; however, with the pressures of NCLB, this cycle has increased. What we do know is that with each suspension the student falls farther and farther behind, grows more frustrated and angry, and will more than likely drop out of school.

NCLB was designed to increase the academic achievement of students from caste/involuntary minority groups but it is these students who are most vulnerable to all negative outcomes associated with it; especially when it comes to exclusionary discipline. Exclusionary discipline in effect works against all of the good intentions for which NCLB was designed. Instead of creating learning environments in which the academic achievement of many students from caste/involuntary minority groups is promoted, it produces another barrier to educational equity.

Perhaps one of the most adverse effects of NCLB has been the neglect of the issue of racial disparity in discipline. The Office of Civil Rights investigation of allegations of discriminatory discipline policies has come to a virtual halt (Witt, 2007). The Office of Civil Rights according to its Annual Report to Congress "has aligned its resources to ensure accomplishment of the goals and objectives in the No Child Left Behind Act." Eliminating racial disparities in school discipline was not listed as a priority in OCR's 2002–2007 Strategic Plan (Office of Civil Rights, 2002).

In the next chapter, we will examine "school-related" factors that contribute to disparity in discipline. These factors come into play with students from all caste/involuntary minority groups. We are often ignorant of the cultures of students from these groups and many times hold "culturally conditioned" beliefs and assumptions about them. As stated earlier, because of the significant numbers of African American students, especially males that are the target of exclusionary discipline, in this chapter we will focus on this group.

RECOMMENDATIONS

Do: Critique a recent discipline event that has occurred in your classroom.

- Describe each aspect of the process (Precipitating Event; Initiation of Disciplinary Event; Progression of Disciplinary Event; Consequences of Disciplinary Event).
- What are the implications?

Chapter 3

Merely a Symptom

What accounts for the disproportionate number of African American students who are referred for disciplinary action? I usually ask this question at the beginning of my workshop on discipline. Generally, I get a rush of hands; responses range from "no discipline at home," "single parent homes," "teenage mothers," "no Black role models," to "television" and "rap music."

I agree with my participants that all of these can be contributing factors and I pose another question: What factors external to the student and his parents or factors inherent in the school environment contribute to the high rates of disciplinary referrals and actions involving African American students? To this question, there is usually no immediate response. After some probing, some brave teacher will usually say "sometimes it's us, our attitudes." With that statement, we can begin the process of addressing the disparity issue.

Disparity in discipline, as indicated by the most recent research findings, is only a symptom of a far more pernicious problem. The focus of this book is on the factors that extend beyond the student, his or her parents, and the family background; the focus is on those factors that are prevalent in the school environment itself that place a student at risk for disciplinary referral and sanctions, and perpetuate racial disparity in discipline.

School-related factors are those beliefs, attitudes, and behaviors that serve as catalysts of interpersonal misunderstandings and conflict, or that cause conflict situations to escalate. School-related factors may also include policies and procedures that leave room for bias. However, teacher and administrator beliefs and attitudes are most associated with disparities in discipline.

Eyler et al. (1983) report that school climate and teacher attitudes are generally associated with disciplinary problems. Positive teacher attitudes about integration are associated with fewer disciplinary problems. It was also found that teachers who supported busing for desegregation perceived a smaller increase in disciplinary problems than teachers who opposed it. Racial disparities in discipline were associated with a lack of administrative support for integration and with school environments that were generally hostile to Black students.

Two school-related factors in particular contribute to disparities in discipline. The first factor is lack of knowledge, understanding, and sensitivity to the culture of African American students. The second school-related factor that negatively affects African American students, especially male students, is the set of faulty assumptions and negative expectations for the academic performance and social behavior of African American students.

Eyler et al. (1983) report that many teachers with socially heterogeneous populations who are confronted with students whose behavior they do not understand subsequently feel ill-equipped to respond or cope with the behavior. The styles of dress and behavior of some Black students may conflict with the teacher's values, resulting in suspensions and discipline problems.

The lack of cultural understanding is most often a problem for non–African American teachers; however, the difference in social class between African American teachers and students may be problematic as well. Furthermore, African American teachers who are more assimilated into mainstream cultural values and beliefs may still experience problems relating to the cultural attributes and styles of their African American students.

Atkinson et al. (1983) describe a model of minority-identity development where minority individuals ideally move from a "conformity" state to one of "self-actualization." African American teachers who are in the conformity state of minority-identity development may (1) identify more strongly with the dominant culture's values, (2) lack awareness of their ethnic perspective, (3) exhibit negative attitudes toward themselves and other African Americans, and (4) accept and believe the prevalent stereotypes about African Americans.

A lack of understanding of, and sensitivity to, the communication style of African American students can create tension between the teacher and student and lead to discipline problems. African Americans tend to be emotional and expressive when communicating. Their volume, tone, and nonverbal movements are often regarded as threatening to a teacher unfamiliar with this style of communicating. Teachers in some desegregated schools recognized that a lack of effective communication with students from cultures different from their own contributes to disciplinary problems (Eyler et al. 1983).

The images of, beliefs about, assumptions of, and expectations for, African American students, especially male students, which are derived from historical stereotypes, contribute in a major way to racial disparities in discipline. The Joint Center for Political Studies (1989) reports that schools institutionalize social inequities through the gross stereotyping of Black children. Negative, inaccurate, and inflexible expectations formed by teachers, based on race and social class, result in the different treatment of minority and White students.

Racial disparities in discipline occur in a larger context in which cultural insensitivity and racial stereotyping combine to create a racially hostile and psychologically unsafe learning environment for African American students.

Hyman and Snook (1999) define emotional maltreatment as any disciplinary or motivational practice that psychologically hurts children. Practices that are considered to be psychological maltreatment in schools are humiliation and denigration; rejection, ignoring, and isolation; authoritarian discipline; sarcasm and put-downs; name calling; ridicule related to intellectual abilities; performance pressures; ridicule related to physical attributes and appearance; and bigotry (both conscious and unconscious) in the classroom.

Daily, many African American students, especially males, enter classrooms in which they are misunderstood and stigmatized. Discipline referrals and sanctions that are the result of cultural insensitivity and unconscious stereotyping occur within school climates that can be considered to be hostile to African American students and, in effect, constitute psychological maltreatment.

One final note: the Office of Civil Rights (1994) considers an educational environment to be hostile when harassing conduct (for example, physical, verbal, graphic, or written) is sufficiently severe, pervasive, or persistent so as to interfere with, or limit the ability of, the student to participate in, or benefit from, the services, activities, or privileges provided by the district.

The Office of Civil Rights also considers students to be the victims of different treatment if behaviors occur (based on the student's race or color) that interfere with or limit the student's ability to participate in, or benefit from, the services, activities, or privileges within the educational setting.

In school environments where cultural insensitivity and unconscious stereotyping are allowed to persist and to influence disciplinary decisions, not only are African American students being psychologically maltreated, but their rights and opportunities to receive an education are being denied as well. Ultimately, racial disparity in discipline must be addressed as a moral, ethical, and legal issue.

Because of the growing number of Hispanic/Latino students in our schools, and the number suspensions that they also experience, in Chapter 4, we will discuss the culture of students from both African American and Latino/Hispanic backgrounds and examine the ways in which culture impacts what happens to them in the classroom.

RECOMMENDATIONS

DO: Review school discipline policies and procedures. Revise any that may leave room for bias.

Part II

Chapter 4

The Impact of Culture

Culture is a group's knowledge and expectations about appropriate modes of interaction and the patterns of activities that are common to that group. The social interactions through which children develop competencies reflect cultural values and standards for appropriate behavior.

According to Greenfield et al. (1996), children come to school acting in accordance with the invisible cultures of their homes and communities, but conflict often arises when their behavior differs from the invisible culture of the school. Three things may occur: the school may devalue and even punish children for behavior their parent's value, teachers may structure classroom interaction patterns that violate the invisible cultural norms of various minority groups, and such conflicts may not be recognized as cultural because of their invisible nature.

By and large, the students who disproportionately receive disciplinary sanctions such as out-of-school suspensions belong to "collectivistic" cultures. Collectivism stresses a "we consciousness"; a collective identity; and fosters interdependence and group success.

The values, style of communication, and ways of being of students from collectivistic cultures differ from that of the school culture which stresses individualism, competition, and individual achievement. Be they Native American, Samoan, African American, or Latino/Hispanic students, their cultural orientation in most instances is at odds with the cultural frame of reference of the school.

In this chapter, we will focus on the cultures of the two groups that are most disproportionately represented among those suspended and expelled from school; African American and Latino/Hispanic students. Many of the cultural attributes that are discussed will also be relevant to other students as well who belong to collectivistic cultures.

AFRICAN AMERICAN STUDENTS

One of the sources of excessive disciplinary referrals is the lack of knowledge of and sensitivity to the culture of African American students. This cultural insensitivity is one of the major complaints I have received from African American parents in the Southern districts in which I work. Comments such as "they are insensitive to African American children" or "they don't know how to work with African American children" are often heard from African American parents.

This insensitivity leads to misinterpretation of, and faulty assumptions about, the behavior of African American students. According to Butler (1992), an appreciation of African American cultural elements is a prerequisite to understanding and interpreting the behavioral patterns of African Americans. In order to decrease disciplinary referrals that result from cultural misunderstandings, teachers and administrators must understand the impact of culture upon the behavior of students.

MYTHS IN RACIAL STEREOTYPING

Although most educators would generally accept the notion that culture influences human behavior, the unique history and status of African Americans in this country poses additional problems to be overcome. Two myths that permeate American popular culture act as a major barrier to understanding and appreciating African American culture.

Both myths, which have existed since Africans were enslaved on these shores, were created and perpetuated to rationalize and justify the enslavement of Africans. These myths are so deeply embedded in the American mind that the author has experienced workshops in which educators are resistant to even discussing the concept of an African American culture, or question its validity or functionality.

Myth #1: African Americans Do Not Have a Culture

Many Americans, even educators, erroneously believe that African Americans arrived from Africa without the benefit of a culture, or that the culture of the enslaved Africans was totally eradicated during the voyage to North America and the process to make Africans accept enslavement.

Beyond that, many people feel that African Americans as a group are simply a poor imitation of Euro-Americans. Although noted anthropologists such as Melville J. Herskovits (1958) have presented cognitive data supporting this fact, the resistance exhibited by many educators when this issue is being discussed indicates that the concept continues to be rejected at an emotional level.

Fact: African Americans Are a Historically and Culturally Distinct Group

Butler (1992) describes African Americans as "a culturally distinct group of people bound by an ideological unity and a functional system of values and beliefs." According to Butler, "despite enslavement, psychological disorientation, social, cultural, and environmental displacement, old cultural patterns have persisted, some have been reinterpreted, others have been syncretized and adapted to fit the environment."

Pinderhughes (1979), cited in Ho (1987), states that the cultural values of African American families are influenced by three major sources: (1) residuals from Africa, (2) identification with mainstream America, and (3) adaptations and responses to minority status.

Myth #2: African Americans Have an Inferior Culture

The second myth acknowledges that African Americans have a distinct culture but that the culture is deficient in some way. The terms "culturally deprived" and "culturally disadvantaged" that were in vogue some years ago alluded to African Americans either being deprived of the traits of the superior Euro-American culture or terribly flawed as a result of having the deficient traits of African American culture.

I felt I came from a rich culture in my small Southern fishing village and was shocked to find that the educational world I was entering as a professional teacher considered me to be culturally deprived. When I conduct workshops and explore the reasons for the behavioral problems that African American student's experience, the response given is often "the poor values [cultural] that the students have learned."

Fact: African American Culture Is Different

African American culture (like that of any other culture) is different from mainstream Euro-American culture but not deficient. First of all, it is a faulty notion to regard one culture as superior to another, as all cultures have norms and practices that meet the needs of the particular group. Secondly, all distinct groups, African Americans included, respond in certain, specific cultural ways.

Butler (1992) describes the core elements that establish the African American's identity and differentiate it from other groups as (1) self-identity, (2) knowledge, (3) emotion, and (4) behavior. Butler suggests that African Americans have distinctive ways of defining who they are and how they acquire knowledge, respond emotionally, and behave.

According to Locke (1992), a number of distinctive characteristics of African American cultural traits give strong credibility to the uniqueness of an African American culture. Locke describes these elements as (1) those not found in the dominant culture, (2) those connected in some way to the traits of other Afrocentric communities, i.e., Caribbean, and (3) those similar to the elements found in West Africa, the location from which most slaves came.

Some distinct differences that Locke found between Western and Afrocentric cultures are differences in the concept of time (relative vs. linear) and the usage of the "be" verb (as illustrated in Black English) to emphasize whether something is done only at the present moment ("She bad") or habitually ("She be bad"). Locke asserts that the society may be that of the United States, but the values are African American, and that African American values come only through an African American culture.

Herskovits (1958) identified a number of cultural elements that are carryovers from Africa and that have survived in the United States. Some of these Africanisms are reflected in the behaviors of today's African American students. These cultural elements are

- Funerals
- Magical practices
- Folklore
- Dance
- Song
- Motor habits (walking, speaking, laughing, sitting, postures, burden-carrying, hoeing, and movements made in various agricultural and industrial activities)
- Ways of dressing hair (wrapping, braiding, cornrowing)
- Wearing of head kerchiefs and scarves
- Etiquette (the use of titles of respect, respect for the elderly, the practice of turning the head when laughing, placing the hand over the mouth, and averting the eyes or turning the face when speaking to respected persons)
- Concept of time (approximations rather than punctuality; CP time; "colored people's time"—habitually arriving late—is culturally expected and accepted)
- Cooperation and sharing (orientation towards collective responsibility and interdependence)

- Child-rearing practices (the use of corporal punishment)
- Adoption of children (informal)
- Myths about abnormal births
- Child-naming practices
- Audience and performer styles (call and response)
- Religious and spiritually expressive styles (highly emotional)
- Conception of the devil

Hillard (1976), cited in Hale-Benson (1986), describes the core of African American cultural style. African Americans tend to

- Respond to things in terms of the whole picture rather than its parts
- Prefer inferential reasoning to deductive or inductive reasoning
- Approximate space, numbers, and time rather than stick to accuracy
- Prefer to focus on people and their activities rather than on things
- Have a keen sense of justice and are quick to analyze and perceive injustice
- Lean toward altruism, a concern for fellow human beings
- Prefer novelty, freedom, and personal distinctiveness (this is shown in the development of improvisations in music and in clothing)
- Not be "word" dependent; African Americans tend to be proficient in nonverbal communication

Lynch and Hanson (1992) contrasted the beliefs, values, and practices of African American and mainstream culture. They found that African American culture is characterized by (1) collective orientation, (2) kinship and extended family bonds, (3) high-context communication, (4) religious and spiritual orientation, (5) more authoritarian childrearing practices, (6) greater respect for the elderly and their role in the family, and (7) more oriented to situation than time.

CULTURAL CONFLICTS IN THE CLASSROOM

Even if the African American student is acknowledged as having a culture, and one that is simply different, not defective, he faces yet another challenge. As Greenfield et al. (1996) suggest, the customary modes of activity and interaction (of minority students) often differ from those favored by the mainstream Euro-American culture in public schools.

Although African Americas are not a monolithic ethnic group, with all members being attached to traditional cultural norms to the same degree, it can be safely stated that African American students generally must give up significant aspects of their cultural identity in order to be successful in the American public school system. Independence and individual achievement, aspects of the core mainstream value of individualism, with Anglo-Saxon and European immigrant origins, is highlighted in the cultural-institutional setting of American schools.

Greenfield et al. (1996) suggest that this contrasts with the collectivistic cultural value orientation (which emphasizes interdependence) of many non-Western immigrants and minority groups, that is, Asian Americans, Hispanics, African Americans, and Native Americans. According to Greenfield et al., children from individualistic and collectivistic value orientations become adept at different modes of activity and have different conceptions of appropriate behavior.

Based upon the author's discussions with teachers and students, there are some cultural patterns that are especially problematic for African American students in the school setting. The behavioral aspects associated with the collectivistic value orientation of African Americans (for example, grouping behavior, the "we," social and cooperative orientations when misunderstood) can be precipitating factors for disciplinary actions involving African American students.

The grouping behavior of African American students can be very threatening and intimidating to some teachers in the school setting. The communalism value is held and practiced very strongly by African American students, especially in situations where they might be in a numerical minority population. It is very important to bond, to stick together, and even to protect each other if necessary.

Sitting together in the cafeteria, at sporting events, and even walking together down the hallways is very important to African American students. This grouping, plus the emotional nature of African American communication (perceived to be loud), often calls attention to African American students. The problem occurs when African American students feel that they are being unduly singled out or harassed when they see other groups engaging in the same behavior.

The "we" orientation is also exhibited in conflict situations. When African American males hear about or see what they believe to be mistreatment or harassment of another African American, especially by an outsider, they assume a protective stance, which often leads to fights.

Not only do African American males feel the obligation to protect other African Americans from students from other groups but from teachers as well, if necessary. African American male students often get into trouble by coming to the defense of another student when they feel the teacher is mistreating or picking on that student. In this situation, the responsibility to the group transcends the individual consequences that may result from this action.

The social orientation of African American students tends to make them appear more interested in socializing than in doing schoolwork. African American students are often written up for wasting time, not completing work, and excessive talking.

This social orientation is most important, however, in the teacher–student relationship. African American students have a high need to connect with the teacher, and to feel that the teacher accepts, respects, and cares about them as individuals. African American students are intuitively aware of the teacher's genuineness and caring. The quality of the teacher–student relationship will determine the extent to which discipline problems will occur with African American students.

The cooperative spirit of African American students is often misinterpreted as cheating. African American students distinguish between actual cheating and helping a friend find the page or "assisting" another student who is having a problem. Other values related to culturally influenced personality traits can also be precipitating factors for conflict in the classroom.

The value of expressive individuality, which is interpreted as style and demonstrated in the fads in clothing, hairstyles, and mannerisms, can cause major problems for African American students. African American males in particular are found to express their individuality in ways that are unacceptable in the school setting.

The wearing of oversized pants, not wearing belts, and the showing of underwear are all unacceptable in the school setting. The wearing of sunglasses and hats indoors, which is inappropriate according to mainstream and school etiquette, is considered totally acceptable by many African American males.

Sometimes, a style of wearing clothing, such as one pant leg up or males wearing cornrows, is incorrectly attributed to gang affiliation. A major cause of conflict between African American students and the administration occurs when students feel they are falsely labeled as gang members.

The concept of social time causes problems for African American students, many of whom are chronically tardy to school or to class. Many African American students move along very slowly when getting to school and to class; the social situation is much more important than the time schedule.

The need for spontaneity and flexibility causes problems, especially for younger African American males, who have difficulty sitting still and attending to one activity for long periods of time. Many young African American males are considered hyperactive and are often referred for special education placement because of their need for activity.

The rigid use of time is a mainstream (European) American value. According to Althen (1988), Americans regard time as a resource, that is, "time is money." The ideal person in this society, in a cultural sense, is one who is punctual and considerate of other people's time.

Althen (1988) concedes that this attitude toward time is not necessarily shared by non-Europeans, who regard time as something around them rather than something to use. He states that one of the most difficult adjustments that many foreign businessmen and students must make in the United States is the notion that time must be saved whenever possible and "used" wisely every day.

The African American relationship to and concept of time has been problematic for them in this country since the enslavement period. According to Sobel (1987), "the use of time was at the heart of owners' criticism of slaves: they wanted slaves to change their perception of time and work."

Time continues to cause problems for African American students. The concept of social time adhered to by many African American students causes them to be chronically late to school or class. I have even experienced this in my own home with two children who were gifted honor students, but who were consistently late because they could not adhere to a rigid time schedule.

It is important, however, for the teacher to distinguish between two groups of tardy students. "Adjustors" (who are adjusting time to fit their social definition) move along slowly, chatting with each other, and enjoying the moment when going to school or class. They are caught up in the moment and regard the social situation as more important than the schedule.

With "avoiders," on the other hand, the focus of being late is to avoid unpleasantness, either because they are unable to perform adequately, or because they expect to have conflict with the teacher.

DEALING WITH TIME ISSUES

1. Realize that the concept of time enforced at school is only one group's way of relating to time. Like other aspects of deep culture, the way one relates to time influences one's view of the world and how to operate in it.
2. Have a dialogue with students about the ways different cultures regard time. Point out that the school culture requires that all students adhere to a rigid time schedule. Explain why punctuality is necessary in the school setting.
3. Allow students to brainstorm ways to incorporate flexibility in the classroom time schedule.
4. Talk to chronically late students; find out why they are late and determine if they are adjustors or avoiders. Use different strategies with each type of student; remember that being late to class is a symptom of a much larger problem for the avoider.

5. Be aware that some conflicts that occur in the classroom may be a rebellion against the rigid adherence to time.
6. Be as flexible as possible with schedules.
7. Give ample warning when changing from one activity to another.
8. Provide sufficient "wait time" for students to respond to questions (at least five seconds); African American males have a tendency to respond more slowly because they want to be absolutely sure of their response.

Dealing with Energetic Students

1. Realize that it is quite normal for boys up to about ages seven or eight to be very energetic.
2. Distinguish between normal high energy and hyperactivity; hyperactivity includes a constellation of symptoms.
3. Release the concept of "controlling" children. Controlling children and teaching children are two very different concepts.
4. Focus on ways to fully engage students with high energy. Direct the energy into creative pursuits.
5. Rather than trying to control the energy, introduce new concepts to challenge the student. Many African American parents tell me that their "high-energy" sons are bored in the classroom.
6. Engage students in more "hands-on" activities.
7. Remember that the optimal attention span for an adult is only twenty minutes. Play activities that allow for ebb and flow, short periods of intense concentration followed by a short break.
8. When high-energy children are grossly involved in an activity, be flexible with time; don't disturb them.
9. Praise high-energy students when they do follow directions.
10. Treat all students the way in which we treat gifted students; we "honor" their quirks.
11. Determine if birth order or other family issues are involved; is the child an only, or the baby, or the only girl, or boy used to attention?
12. Recommend parenting skills, if warranted.

Another value that causes the most problems for African American students is that of the need for fairness, equality, and justice. African American students are keenly aware of unfairness; they are always vigilant, and analyze situations to determine if injustice has occurred. In this respect, African American males have a great need to be heard and to explain their side.

Most often, conflicts occur and incidents escalate because the African American male student feels that he either (1) was not taken seriously, (2) was not listened to, or (3) was not given the opportunity to tell his side. When any of these three events occurs, the African American male will persist in talking to be heard or to state his case.

Unless the teacher listens, this situation will build to a point where the student (in the words of African American male students) "snaps" or "goes off on the teacher." Many African American male students feel that this is the only way that they can get a teacher to really listen to them.

In a society in which many African American males feel a very fragile connection and future, their culture is all they have. Adolescent African American males attach very strongly to the values of communalism, expressive individuality, and justice. Their walk, their speech, their mannerisms, and their interactions will express these values. These values help to define their identity and to provide some level of stability in what otherwise might be perceived as a very precarious life situation.

HISPANIC/LATINO STUDENTS

Hispanic/Latino students face similar issues related to discipline and cultural differences as African American students. The concepts and strategies described here can be beneficial to administrators and teachers who work with Hispanic/Latino students. It is important that educators consider these issues for several reasons.

First, demographic studies indicate that Hispanics/Latinos will account for 44 percent of the nation's population growth between 1995 and 2025. The most pronounced development in school demographics has been in the growth of Latino/Hispanic students. In 2005, Latino/Hispanics made up one fifth of public school students.

Second, current data indicates that, like African American students, Hispanic/Latino students are suspended and expelled from public schools at higher rates than their White counterparts. New federal findings showed that Hispanic/Latino students accounted for 14 percent of the suspensions and 16 percent of the expulsions (Johnston, 2000). According to the Advancement and Civil Rights Projects at Harvard University (2000), like African American students

1. Zero tolerance policies are more likely to exist in predominately Latino school districts than in predominately White school districts.
2. Latino children are more likely to be referred for disciplinary action and to be disciplined than are White children.

3. Latino children are more likely to be disciplined for minor misconduct and receive punishments disproportionate to their conduct than are White students.
4. Latino children are more likely to be suspended for "discretionary" offenses than are their White counterparts.

Third, like African American students, Hispanic/Latino students may bring cultural beliefs, values, practices, and communication patterns that are different from the mainstream orientation advocated in our schools. Ho (1987) describes five common cultural values that significantly influence Hispanic/Latino life: familism, personalismo, hierarchy, spiritualism, and fatalism.

The value of personalismo is described as that by which a Hispanic/Latino defines his self-worth in terms of those inner qualities that give him self-respect and earn him the respect of others. "He feels an inner dignity (dignidad) and expects others to show respect (respecto) for that dignidad."

Closely related to the concept of personalismo is the quality of machismo or maleness. Machismo is that quality of personal magnetism that impresses or influences others; it is a style of personal daring by which one faces challenges, danger, and threats with calmness and self-possession. It would appear that these two values, in particular, personalismo and machismo, if not fully understood or misunderstood, could create tension and conflict between the teacher and especially the Hispanic/Latino male student who espouses these values.

Zuniga (1992) points out that Latino cultures value (1) a collective orientation, (2) interdependence, (3) a collective group identity, (4) cooperation, 5) saving face, (6) emphasis on interpersonal relations, and (7) a relaxed time orientation. These values are in direct contrast to the mainstream cultural values of an individual orientation, independence, individual identity, competition, being direct, emphasis on task orientation, and time sensitivity.

This contrast in core cultural values is another area in which the lack of cultural understanding or the lack of appreciation of the cultural values could possibly lead to conflict in the classroom and subsequent discipline problems. Also, differences in the communication style of the Hispanic/Latino student and the mainstream teacher (for example, showing respect by looking down) can be problematic.

Locke (1992) states that Mexican Americans engage in verbal play. They rely heavily on jokes, jocular talking, and in-group humor to relieve tension and stress. Like African American males, this type of verbal play may not be understood or appreciated and may present problems for Mexican American students.

Finally, it is important to acknowledge the differences between the different groups constituting "Hispanics." Hispanic Americans are also known as Chicanos, Latinos, Mexicans, Hispanic, Spanish-speaking Americans, Spanish Americans, and Spanish-surnamed Americans (Ho, 1987).

It is also important to recognize that the different groups of Hispanics may have entirely different school experiences based upon their status and value in American society. Cubans and other South or Central American émigrés, though they may be political refugees, are considered voluntary immigrants and immigrant minorities. Mexican American and Puerto Rican students' school experiences will most closely mirror those of African American students.

Locke (1992) describes Mexican Americans as a group, shut off from the usual avenues of achievement by prejudice and discrimination. Like African Americans, they are plagued by damaging stereotypes (for example, Mexicans are lazy, passive, and failure oriented).

Although Puerto Ricans are the only immigrants who come to the main-land of the United States as citizens of this country, they are an extremely devalued group (Locke, 1992). Younger Puerto Ricans who have grown up in low-income urban communities face the most problems. Like Mexican Americans, they are portrayed in a negative manner by the media. They lack a strong sense of cultural identity, and suffer from racial ambiguity that results in conflict between them and the dominant culture.

Like African American students, Mexican American and Puerto Rican students attend schools that are microcosms of the larger society. Mexican American and Puerto Rican students in particular may be more vulnerable to factors in the school environment, such as the lack of cultural understanding and stereotyping that contribute to their disproportional representation in discipline statistics.

The same approaches described in this book to eliminate racial disparities in discipline, as they pertain to African American students, can be adapted for use in schools with predominately Hispanic/Latino populations.

TEN WAYS TO DECREASE CONFLICTS RELATED TO CULTURAL DIFFERENCES IN THE CLASSROOM

1. Realize that the denial and devaluation of the culture of African American students is cultural racism (see Lustig and Koester, 1996).
2. Ask: "What works in a culturally diverse school environment so that the norms of all ethnic groups are to some extent acknowledged and respected?"

3. Facilitate dialogues on cultural attributes and identity so that students can distinguish traditional positive cultural practices (collectivism) from negative cultural practices, for example, the wearing of pants with no belts (from the prison culture).
4. Facilitate dialogues that distinguish between stereotypes (which originate outside the group and are used to control the group) and cultural attributes (which come from the group itself and are used to meet the needs of the group).
5. Don't be quick to accuse students of cheating; you may be seeing an innocent display of cooperation.
6. Let students help determine classroom rules and school discipline codes.
7. Always leave room for negotiation.
8. Seek input from parents and individuals from the community regarding the issue of cultural differences and discipline.
9. Refrain from assuming that all the negative behaviors exhibited by African American students are aspects of traditional African American culture.
10. Incorporate some collectivistic values and practices in the classroom, for example, peer tutoring, cooperative learning activities, and whole-class teaching.

In the next chapter, we will deal with the aspect of culture that causes the most problems for African American students in the classroom; their communication style. It should be noted that some of the cultural preferences in communication styles will also be relevant to other students from collective cultures, i.e., eye contact, emotional expression, etc.

RECOMMENDATIONS

Do: Invite *cultural informants* (parents or community members from the African American and/or Hispanic/Latino cultural groups) to talk to the faculty/staff about the group's culture and experiences as a minority in this society.

Chapter 5

Cross-Cultural Communication Conflicts in the Classroom

African American culture is an oral culture. Great significance is placed on the oral transmission of information. Traditionally, African beliefs, values, customs, and history were transmitted by word of mouth from generation to generation. In African American culture, great respect is afforded those who possess exceptional verbal skills. If one examines the leaders whom African Americans have chosen to listen to, they are, without exception, great orators.

The significance placed on oral skill in African American culture is so important that a major part of the socialization process, especially for African American males ages eight to fifteen, is the rite of passage associated with learning and using the language of the culture.

According to Hale-Benson (1986), an important manhood rite for African American males is playing the dozens, an activity engaged in primarily by young men in which two opponents dual verbally. Derogatory comments are made about each other, and their respective family members, especially the mother. The successful player masters several competencies, including being able to think quickly, and to control his emotions. This culturally approved and respected verbal skill causes special problems for African American males in the school setting.

According to Dandy (1991), (1) African American males speak a particular kind of stylized talk, (2) learning how to use this talk is an essential part of passage from boyhood to manhood, (3) teachers generally are unfamiliar with the rules, purpose, and intent of this stylized talk, and (4) often the students who use this talk are referred by teachers to remedial classes, special education classes, or classes for behavior disorders. The manner and tone in which some African American male students, in particular, communicate is often considered to be disrespectful and even intimidating by some teachers.

CULTURALLY BASED COMMUNICATION PREFERENCES AND TABOOS

Each of the following communication preferences or taboos can create tension and cause conflict if not understood and respected.

Call and Response

This communication pattern is seen in African American churches when African Americans listen to speakers. It is permissible and expected that one respond verbally to a speaker; this usually indicates approval for what the speaker is saying and encourages the speaker to continue in the same vein. For instance, in church, it is permissible to say "Amen" or "say it" back to the preacher. When African Americans hear the speaker say something that they like, it is permissible to say "tell it like it is" or something similar to encourage the speaker.

I always smile to myself when the "silence is golden" appears on the movie screen. It doesn't have the same impact for some African American moviegoers who customarily "talk back to the characters on the screen." One might hear "You tell him, girl!" or "Don't go in there!" to warn a character in the movie. Verbal disapproval is also allowed in some settings, for instance, at talent shows, where the audience indicates its disapproval through hoots, grunts, and the like.

This African American cultural form is foreign to and disapproved of in the school setting. The school rule is to sit quietly and listen to the speaker. Interrupting the speaker with encouraging as well as disapproving remarks is taboo. African American students who "forget where they are" and respond in this manner are considered to be rude and out of line. The student's response and feeling on the other hand, is "All I said was . . ." He then feels angry and that the teacher is "picking on him."

Distance

The relationship that one has with an African American determines how close one gets to him or her in a conversation. Individuals from outside the culture are usually not permitted to get as close unless a relationship exists with that person. In a conflict situation, it is appropriate to maintain a distance of at least three feet or arm's length. The comment "don't get in my face" indicates that one is violating an individual's space.

Often, in order to show power and authority, a teacher will get into an African American male student's face. This is a major cultural taboo for

African Americans; it is considered a challenge and will be treated as such. If the teacher does not respond to the student's warning to get out of his face, then the student will probably resort to some physical means to protect his "space."

Physical Contact

In the midst of a conflict, any movement touching the other individual is considered provocation. Two African American individuals may engage in a loud and very emotional argument, but may be nowhere near fighting unless one of them makes a provocative move. This move is usually an indication that one must protect oneself. When teachers touch or push or move students along, the student's response is usually "don't touch me." In some cases, the student will view the touching as provocation and respond in a physical manner. Again, as in the case of distance, a "relationship" will make the difference.

Eye Contact

Traditionally, African American children have been taught to lower the gaze to show respect and humility for parents and other adults. To stare at an adult is considered rude and is taboo. There are some African American parents today, however, who teach their children to hold their heads up and look every one in the eye as a means of maintaining their dignity.

A problem arises when the teacher attempts to force an African American male to make eye contact when the student was taught to lower the gaze to show respect. Contrary to the belief of some teachers, an African American male's lowering of the eyes does not mean that he is lying or trying to hide something. It also is not an indication of low self-esteem in this instance.

Many teachers who need to exert their power through attempting to force eye contact insist that they only do this because African American males must learn to establish eye contact in the job market. It is very important to separate the two; forcing a student to make eye contact in a conflict situation is not the same situation as a job interview, and can only lead to an escalation of the conflict.

Gestures

African Americans find the direct pointing of fingers to show authority, and finger-snapping to get one to move, to be inappropriate. When a teacher puts his or her finger in the face of an African American male, or snaps fingers to move him along, it is considered insulting, and the student will usually respond.

Emotional Expression

African Americans are "high-keyed" communicators, which means we are loud and emotional when talking about something that we are very interested in or have strong feelings about. When talking about something that is very important to us, we become very excited and animated. When we are engaging in a debate, we may express our opinions in a loud and emotional manner, even though we are not angry. Many times, outsiders to the African American culture may feel that we are venting anger or hostility when they hear us arguing a point.

The loud and emotional manner in which African American males communicate is very threatening and intimidating to teachers who do not understand this communication style. Teachers will often send students to the office because they fear a fight is going to break out, when in actuality the students are only engaging in a verbal game of "sellin' wolf tickets" (loud threats).

When African American males and teachers are involved in a conflict situation, especially when the male feels he has been unjustly accused or has not been able to state his case, he may become louder and more animated. This is not an indication that he is ready to strike the teacher, only that he is trying harder "to be heard."

High-Context Communication

African Americans are known as high-context communicators. We are not "word-bound," and as such, derive as much meaning from what is not said verbally (the nonverbal cues) as from what is stated. African Americans watch the facial expressions, body movements, the stance, and even the changes in complexion when assessing a situation. African Americans place a high value on being genuine and "real," and use the nonverbal cues as indicators of genuineness.

When an African American student says that a particular teacher does not like him or that a teacher is prejudiced, he is usually basing his beliefs on intuitive feelings and nonverbal cues. This, of course, often makes the African American student appear as though he is using "race as an excuse," because members of mainstream culture tend to utilize information obtained from words and the senses (rather than intuition) to make judgments.

CULTURAL TABOOS

Asking personal questions, shaming in public, and the use of the terms "boy," "girl," and "you people" are highly offensive to African Americans of any age. African Americans have a concept of "my business," and are often suspicious when individuals appear to be too interested in their personal lives. "Boy," "girl," and "you people" are considered derogatory terms. Young African American males find "boy" to be particularly offensive and will confront a teacher whom she or he is talking to if addressed as "boy."

Public shaming is a definite taboo; when an African American male is shamed in front of his classmates, he will take the shaming as a challenge as well as an insult, and will defend both his manhood and his dignity. Public shaming on the part of a teacher can only lead to a "lose–lose" situation. The student will invariably be punished for the outbreak that will occur after the incident, and the teacher will lose the trust and respect of the other students who observed the incident.

If teachers can become aware of and respect the cultural rules relating to communication styles, tension between teachers and African American male students will decrease; conflicts can be avoided and incidents will not escalate.

CULTURAL ETIQUETTE

The social forms to be observed in interactions with individuals from diverse cultural backgrounds are cultural etiquette. There are rules that govern all of our interactions with others, and rules for interacting with those who may come from backgrounds different from our own. What follows are some rules for interacting with African American males in the classroom, especially in conflict situations. When teachers follow these rules, they show a respect for the culture, the communication preferences, and taboos of African American students. These rules relate to each of the communication elements previously discussed.

Call and Response

Do explain that there are different types of responses that are appropriate for different kinds of activities. Allow students to establish rules for when a more culturally based style can be used—for example, when discussing current events or some political issue.

Distance

Do not get in his face. Maintain an acceptable distance (about an arm's length), especially when in the midst of a conflict.

Physical Contact

Do not touch him, especially in the middle of a conflict situation. If he needs to leave the room, give a friend permission to walk outside the room with him, and talk to him until he cools down (all with the student's permission, of course).

Eye Contact

Don't force him to establish eye contact. His not looking at you does not necessarily mean that he is lying, trying to hide something, or being defiant.

Gestures

Do not point your finger in his face or snap your fingers at him.

Emotional Expression

Do not assume that he is going to hit you or someone else if he is loud and animated. Most importantly, give him the opportunity to be heard, to defend himself, and to state his case. Doing this simple thing will decrease conflict with African American males to a significant extent. Also, learn to distinguish when he is strongly expressing an opinion or arguing the "principle of the thing" from when he is angry.

High-Context Communication

Listen to him when he says that he feels that you don't like him. Don't become defensive if he says that he feels you are prejudiced. Ask him what makes him feel this way. Do some self-reflection and determine how you feel about him and why.

CULTURAL TABOOS

Never call him "boy." Most importantly, never shame him in public. Ask him to step aside or right outside the door to speak to him. Ask him if you two can spend some quality time talking about the issue later so that the problem can be resolved.

Use the SSS method: the first "S" is "stroke," the second "S" is "sting," and the third "S" is "stroke" again. First, say something positive about the student; next, indicate your disappointment in his behavior; then say something positive about the student again and your hopes for behavior that is more like the person that you know that he really is or can be. This technique can get a point across while defusing a situation; I have used it and it works!

AVOIDING THE ESCALATION OF DISCIPLINE EVENTS

A "perceived insult" is often the precipitating factor when a miscommunication escalates into a full-blown discipline event. The student, usually an African American male, perceives that he or a classmate has been insulted or disrespected by the teacher. The violation of some cultural norm is usually what causes the student to react; he feels that he must defend his honor or that of a classmate.

When African American males are asked how a particular situation could have been avoided, they often respond: "If she had just asked me to be quiet, she didn't have to yell at me"; or "Why did he have to get in my face?" Sometimes a student reacts to repeated admonitions to "look at me!"

The cultural violation, the student's perception, and his defense set into motion an event that escalates and ends with the student being sent to out of school suspension (OSS) or worse depending upon the level to which the event escalates. A typical event that escalates follows:

- Teacher: (Yells at student) "I told you to sit down!"
- Student: "Why you got to yell at me?" (Other students laugh)
- Teacher: (Disregarding student's response, yells again) "Sit down mister! "I'm not telling you again."
- Student: "Why you acting like that? What's wrong with you? Don't you see me going to my seat?"
- Teacher: "That's it buddy, you are out of here." (Approaches student to move him along)
- Student: "Get your hands off me!"
- Teacher: "What did you say to me? Who do you think you are talking to?"
- Student: "I said keep your hands off me."
- Teacher; (Angered by student response and starting to feel threatened) Calls for officer to come and take student from room.
- Student: "I didn't do nothing, you jokey."
- Teacher: "I'll add that to your referral. You are out of here."
- Student: F___ you!

The escalation of this event could have been avoided by the teacher adhering to cultural rules that governed the communication with this student. Yelling at him, ignoring his comments, and approaching him all helped to escalate the event.

The term "you jokey," used by students at a high school in which I observed, means "you can't be serious," and is taken very personally by teachers. Students frequently use the term and are just as often sent to in school suspension (ISS) for its use.

Perceived insult or disrespect is a very sensitive issue for African American male students, especially those in adolescence. Their mantra has come to be "I'll respect him or her if they respect me." Many African American males in particular have felt disrespected throughout their school careers. A teacher's reaction and communication with a student can either de-escalate or escalate a discipline event. The teacher's understanding of the African American males feelings in this regard and a respect for cultural norms of communication can go far in preventing events from escalating.

If teachers will follow the communication guidelines described above, then classroom conflicts will decrease. After all, our goal is not to simply punish students, but to teach them more appropriate ways in which to behave and to prevent conflict and the escalation of incidents. When students get into trouble, they are not in class or in school; each day they are not in class or in school, they fall farther behind and their chances for academic success decreases.

In Chapter 6, we examine the issue of stereotyping especially as it relates to the African American male. Unconscious stereotyping leads to unwarranted and excessive referrals of African American male students. Unfortunately, even good teachers can hold and act upon stereotypes of African American males.

RECOMMENDATIONS

Do: Observe your feelings and behaviors when interacting with African American students.

- Determine what you can do to ease any tension that exists between you and African students, especially males.
- Determine how you can prevent discipline events from escalating.

Chapter 6

Stereotyping in the Classroom

I have spent the last ten years going in and out of classrooms and school districts in an effort to ensure that all students have access to the best possible educational opportunities and are treated fairly. Over these ten years, two things have become glaringly apparent to me: first, stereotypes are pervasive in the school environment; and second, the lives of students are affected in a major way as the result of stereotyping. Specifically, I have observed that

- Stereotypes shape the beliefs and behaviors of teachers and administrators.
- These stereotypes influence the relationships that students have with teachers and administrators, as well as the educational outcomes of students, especially as related to academic placement and discipline.
- These stereotypes most often operate at a programmed, unconscious level and generate an automatic response.
- The most pervasive, persistent, and negative stereotypes are attached to the African American male student.

Although the lack of knowledge and understanding of the culture of African American male students places them at risk for disciplinary actions, the problems that African American students, especially males, experience in the school setting are equally the result of faulty assumptions and erroneous beliefs based upon historical myths and stereotypes. These myths and stereotypes generate fear and the need to exercise absolute control in the minds of many teachers, especially non–African American female teachers, and create a vicious cycle from which African American male students in particular cannot escape.

THE NATURE OF STEREOTYPES

Boskin (1970) states that a stereotype is a standardized mental picture representing an oversimplified opinion or an uncritical judgment that is tenacious in its hold over rational thinking. He further describes stereotypes as

- Being pervasive once implanted in the popular lore
- An integral part of the pattern of culture which operates within and at most levels of society
- Affecting thoughts and actions at both conscious and unconscious levels
- Operating at reactive levels of thought and action
- Receiving power from repetition
- Very powerful, "often so powerful that they can be dislodged only after a series of assaults on them"

These stereotypical images over time become part of the cultural fabric of the society. They become central to the thinking and behavior of the mainstream society towards the targeted group. Most significantly, the erroneous beliefs that result from these images are generally accepted as truth, they are not questioned, and they remain as part of the core belief structure of the larger society, unless changed at an institutional level by the leadership, decree, or mandate. By and large, anyone who grows up in the society is influenced by these beliefs.

THE CULTURAL CONDITIONING PROCESS

According to Paul (1998) and Loewenberg (1970), we are culturally conditioned to develop a set of erroneous beliefs based on stereotypes. This is how the process occurs: as children, we are born "tabula rasa" or "clean slate"; we learn what we are to believe about others from our environment; then we receive messages from significant and powerful others that help us form our belief system.

We receive messages from our parents, grandparents, aunts, and uncles—all the people whom we love and respect. When they tell us that a certain group of people is different from us, not as good as us, not to be trusted, or to be avoided, we usually believe them, because these are people that we trust, people who take care of us and meet our needs.

We also receive many significant messages through the social learning context; everything does not have to be stated verbally. Non–African American children are taught to fear Blacks when they are told to check the security of their car doors when they see a group of African American males walking on the street. Anyone who grew up with the Aunt Jemima or Uncle Mose salt-and-pepper shakers learned a lesson, never stated verbally, about the subservient role of African Americans.

By the same token, if the individuals that we are told to respect and honor because they are heroes and leaders give us messages about certain groups through their speeches or writings, those messages also become part of our belief system. When Thomas Jefferson, the quintessential American hero, wrote of the inferiority of Blacks, his message became central to the belief system regarding the treatment of Blacks in this society.

These erroneous beliefs based upon stereotypes are transmitted from generation to generation. Unless the cycle is broken, by an individual or by decree, stereotypical beliefs are passed verbally and nonverbally from one generation to another. Unless corrected, children will hold the same beliefs as their parents and grandparents. Also, unless corrected, generations of students will develop beliefs from textbooks and history lessons based upon myths and stereotypes.

These erroneous beliefs become imprinted at a very early age. By age five or earlier, beliefs based on myths and stereotypes are already developed.

Eventually, these erroneous beliefs operate at a programmed unconscious level and generate an automatic response. In most instances, when we are reacting to an individual on the basis of a stereotype, we are unaware of it. This unconscious, programmed nature of stereotypes makes them so difficult to change.

Modifying erroneous beliefs will occur only through examining these beliefs at a conscious level, monitoring one's behavior, and practicing positive conscious beliefs.

STEREOTYPICAL IMAGES OF AFRICAN AMERICANS

Stereotypical images of African Americans have existed since the enslavement of African peoples in this country, and have become as American as apple pie. These images have played a major role in defining American culture and are a significant part of the American cultural belief system.

Rome (1998) states that the earlier belief of African slaves as inferior to Whites is very important to understanding stereotypes, because it shapes the ways in which African Americans are perceived today. He states further that it is important to understand the unique experience of African Americans in

Table 6.1.   List of Stereotypes

Stereotypes of African Americans

1.

2.

3.

4.

5.

6.

7.

8.

9.

10.

American history. No other group entered as slaves, and just as important, no other group has been victimized "across centuries" like African Americans because of the original enslaved status.

Before I talk about these images further, I would like for you, the reader, to take an active role in this discussion. In the space provided in table 6-1 (or on a separate sheet of paper), I would like you to list the stereotypes that you have either heard of or are aware of that are attributed to African Americans, both male and female. List as many stereotypes as you can, but don't stop writing until you have a minimum of ten.

How did you feel as you completed this exercise? Acknowledging rather than denying the existence of stereotypes is the first step in their eradication. I have had many teachers become very uncomfortable when they are simply asked to list the stereotypes that they have "heard or of which they are aware." I often have to point out that I am not asking if they hold the stereotypes, but rather just to list them.

If you found this activity to be very uncomfortable, then I would say that you should give close attention to this and the following chapters.

Below are some of the stereotypes that are commonly attributed to African Americans. Which ones were on your list?

inferior	lazy	culturally deprived
irresponsible	musical, have rhythm	on welfare
athletic	criminal	drug abusers
intellectually inferior	violent	dishonest
drug dealers	sexually endowed/active	

Now look at another list of stereotypes of African Americans. Check off the ones that in some form or another are the same or are similar to the stereotypes that you listed.

the savage African
the happy slave
the devoted servant
the corrupt politician
the irresponsible
the petty thief
the social delinquent
the vicious criminal
the sexual superman
the superior athlete

the unhappy non-White
the natural-born cook
the natural-born musician
the perfect entertainer
the superstitious churchgoer/citizen
the chicken and watermelon eater
the razor and knife "toter"
the uninhibited expressionist
the mentally inferior

You probably listed or have at least heard some form of many of the stereotypes on this list. What is significant about this list is that it is entitled The Nineteen Basic Stereotypes of Blacks in American Society and was compiled by L. D. Reddick in The Journal of Negro Education in 1944. As you can see, stereotypes of African Americans are of a persistent and consistent nature.

THE CREATION OF THE STEREOTYPICAL BLACK

The discussion of racial stereotyping is an emotional, sensitive, and often uncomfortable topic. We are victims of a cultural conditioning process that we do not understand, nor do we know its origins. If we as educators are going to eliminate the deleterious effects of stereotyping in the classrooms, we must fully understand how and why stereotypes are created and perpetuated.

First of all, stereotypes are never innocent creations; they always serve a deliberate purpose. In the case of African Americans, stereotypes were created to justify the institution of slavery and to rationalize the contradiction inherent in its existence in an otherwise free society (Bireda, 2000).

Oliver (1998) asserts that since Black people were brought to America in 1619 as slaves, derogatory words have been used to construct an American image of Black people as being innately lazy, ignorant, crime prone, promiscuous, and irresponsible. The linguistic stigmatization of Black people and the subsequent distortion of their image as a people have been used to rationalize discrimination toward them.

During various periods in American history, such as during the abolition of slavery in the North, after the Emancipation of slaves, during Reconstruction, and especially from the 1880s to the 1930s, negative images of Blacks influenced race relations by justifying discrimination and violence toward African Americans. At significant junctures in America's history, stereotypical images of African Americans have emerged to shape public attitudes toward them. The dominant caricatures of Blacks in American life are presented in Table 6.2.

Stereotypical images of African Americans have historically been transmitted through five major sources: religion, history, social science, popular culture (ethnic notions), and the media. According to Newby (1965), in the three decades following the Spanish-American War, anti-Negro racism developed on two levels. The first consisted of systematic ideas developed by scientists, social scientists, historians, and religious leaders—groups who endeavored to create a racist ideology supported by scientific, historical, and/or religious authority.

At the second level, popular attitudes were formulated and expounded by journalists, politicians, and popularizers—groups who were concerned with molding or reflecting popular opinion. The images created by both groups were reflected in attitudes and policies, both national and sectional, toward African Americans.

For almost four hundred years, stereotypical images of African Americans have flourished in American society. Because of their tenacity and emotional appeal, stereotypes of African Americans have endured and have been reinforced in major societal institutions. Unfortunately, but understandably, our schools, as microcosms of society, harbor the same stereotypes of African Americans.

The beliefs about and attitudes toward African Americans that are prevalent in the larger society exist in the school setting as well. Since stereotypical

Table 6.2. Dominant Caricatures of Blacks

Sociopolitical period	Image	Purpose
Slavery	Mammy, Coon, Sambo, Tom, Picaninny	To justify slavery; soothe White consciences
Emancipation; Reconstruction World War II	Black Peril, Brute, lazy, dishonest, immoral	To justify violence; to eliminate economic competition
Civil Rights Movement; Black Power Movement, 1950s–1970s	menace, anti-White, aggressive	To discount and neutralize black activism
New Racism (subtle vs. open racism); Retreat from the issue of race, 1980s–2001	criminal, drug dealer, welfare queen, gang-banger	To halt black economic and social progress

images of African Americans are part of the cultural psyche of America, and operate at a programmed unconscious level, administrators, and teachers (yes, even good teachers) may respond at an unconscious level to a stereotype. Becoming a teacher does not undo the years of cultural conditioning that all of us undergo.

THE MYTHICAL AFRICAN AMERICAN MALE

The most vicious, pervasive, and enduring stereotypes were attributed to African American males (Bireda, 2000). Boskin (1986) describes two predominant images of African American men that were developed and flourished almost simultaneously for almost four hundred years: Sambo and the Brute. Both images were derived from the view of African Americans as inferior (for religious, biological, anthropological, or historical reasons) and both images were originated by White Americans and were utilized as a means of maintaining their superior position in society.

Sambo was principally utilized to present a benign portrait of slavery. Sambo had two principal parts to his nature: he was both childish and comical. Above all, Sambo was very amenable to enslavement and to second-class citizenship. This image of the African American male was that of a natural slave-servant. He was nonviolent and humble. He most often played the role of buffoon, displaying outlandish gestures and physical gyrations.

The Sambo image also portrayed the African American male as docile, irresponsible, unmanly, servile, grinning, happy-go-lucky, dependent, slow-witted, humorous, childlike, spiritual singing, and of course, watermelon-eating and chicken-stealing. Sambo was an image of the African American male that provided a measure of psychological safety and security. As long as African American males identified with the image of Sambo, they were considered to be nonthreatening and were safe from harm to a certain extent.

The Sambo caricature, portrayed as the silly, stupid clown who was afraid of the dark, who was happy despite his condition, who was ever grateful for the paternalism of the enslaver, and who even defended slavery, was created during the early years of slavery and was intensified during the period when slavery was abolished in the North.

With Emancipation and Reconstruction came a new, more threatening image of the African American male: the Brute was born. African American males were portrayed as ignorant, corrupt legislators who stole government money, who pushed Whites off sidewalks, and as sexual predators that lusted after White women. In addition, the Brute, because of his violent nature, was thought to be prone to rioting and fighting. The image of the Brute created fear and the need to control the African American male.

The images of the athletic and rhythm-filled African American had their roots in the enslavement period as well. The role that the enslaved were required to fulfill next to that of being a laborer or a servant was that of the entertainer. Enslaved Africans were forced to dance on the slave ships (to exercise the enslaved) and on the auction blocks. On the plantation, dancing, singing, and playing musical instruments were encouraged, rewarded, and often demanded.

Athletics emerged as another aspect of entertainment (Boskin, 1986). Enslaved men were often bet upon as they participated in sporting events such as bareback jockeys, boxers, wrestlers, and foot racers. Like the images of the dependent, irresponsible, corrupt, thieving, and violent African American male, the images of the super athlete and entertainer have endured for almost four hundred years as well.

All of these images, as well as other images, were borne out of a particular historical context and were created to justify the status and treatment of African American males. Unfortunately, some variety of these same stereotypes survive today and continue to negatively affect young African American males in all aspects of society, from "driving while Black" to disparities in school discipline.

When unconscious stereotyping of African American males occurs in the school setting, it produces faulty assumptions, false accusations, and fear of the African American male student. The resultant tension, misunderstandings, miscommunication, and conflict make it impossible for the African American male students and their teachers to develop rapport or workable relationships. Most often, African American male students become trapped in a cycle of alienation that spirals from disciplinary referrals to suspensions and expulsions to academic failure and dropping out (Bireda, 2000).

THE NEED FOR RELATIONSHIP

One of the most effective ways to reduce disciplinary events in the classroom is to establish authentic relationships with African American male students. Because of the pervasiveness of stereotyping, African American males are the most intimidating and feared of all students. It is African American male students who need relationships with teachers most, but who are the least likely to have those relationships.

I held a series of workshops with both African American male and female students in a predominately African American high school. The males were very suspicious and slow to warm. As African American males progress through the grades, they sense that they are treated differently and unfairly; their anger and resentment toward the "system" grows. By the time they reach secondary school, many are so distrustful that it takes great effort to reach them.

A major turning point in our relationship came when we did a session on stereotyping. Some boys who had been very reserved opened up and some who had previously played around took an interest in the session. In fact, they rated the session on stereotyping as the best session. What I think happened is that for the first time, these young men recognized that I really understood them (at least as much as I could not being an African American male myself) and what they endured being African American males. One of the things that African American males need most is to feel that they are listened to and understood.

To start the relationship-building process with African American male students

- Try to really understand what it is like to live under the yoke of negative stereotyping.
- Recognize that much of their anger and resentment (displayed as "defiant" behavior) comes from the knowledge that they have been, are, and will be treated differently in this society.
- Engage them in a conversation about what it means to them to be an African American male.
- Really listen to them; not only their words but their feelings.
- Take a personal interest in them.
- Take an interest in the "whole" person, not just academics.
- Explore with him his talents and abilities.
- Constantly verbalize your high expectations for him.
- Let him know through your actions toward him that you do not believe the stereotypes about African American males.

Poverty, family problems, low academic skills, and personal issues can and do precipitate student acting out. You can lessen the extent to which these events occur and escalate in your classroom by building relationships with your African American male students. In the next chapter, we will discuss the ways in which cultural miscommunication and unconscious stereotyping leads to racial disparity in discipline. If we truly want to decrease disciplinary events in our classrooms, then we must be mindful of those "school-related" factors that promote these events.

RECOMMENDATIONS

Do: Begin the relationship-building process with the African American males
with whom you teach.

- Remember that the students who give you the most trouble are those most
  in need of a relationship with you.

Chapter 7

Cultural Conflicts, Cultural Conditioning, and Disciplinary Practices

The interaction of cultural misunderstanding and unconscious stereotypes affects the relationships between African American students and their teachers, and increases the risk that African American students will receive disciplinary referrals and sanctions. The lack of cultural understanding affects the discipline process in several ways.

First of all, misperceptions occur in two ways: what is interpreted as misbehavior (for example, heads lowered and eyes cast down in humility) is viewed as defiance; the behavior is judged solely on the basis of the teacher's own cultural standards (for example, the raising of the voice in an effort to persuade versus being an aggressive act).

Secondly, projection may occur. In that case, since the teacher does not have accurate information on which to base behavioral interpretations, the only available information (that from culturally conditioned stereotypes) is used to make a judgment. Finally, inappropriate expectations, or lowered or extremely high expectations, can be held for the behavior of African American students.

When unconscious stereotyping occurs in the school setting, faulty assumptions, false accusations, and fear are commonplace. Miscommunication takes place, tension mounts, and conflicts between teachers and African American students result.

Stereotyping most often produces predictable results in the form of self-fulfilling prophecies, and always leads to tension and conflict in the classroom. First, in most instances, at an unconscious level, the teacher or administrator holds a stereotypical image and related erroneous belief about the African American student. Second, an event occurs in the classroom that elicits an automatic response from the teacher. Third, this response elicits an immediate reaction from the student. Fourth, the student's reaction confirms the belief held about the student and reinforces the stereotype.

The comments of one principal are an indication of the type of interactions that occur with African American students. When an African American male was given a referral, the principal remarked with obvious glee, "Ah ha! We've got him now." She had been annoyed for some time by what she considered his defiant attitude. The student was enraged by the principal's comment and proceeded to tell her so. The more the student vented, the more vindicated the principal felt. The student was now proving what she had always believed.

As was stated earlier, African American male students, in particular, are the victims of differential treatment that occurs because of stereotyping. They face similar experiences in school, as do older African American males in the larger society.

If we fear African American males on the streets, we fear them in the hallways; if we follow African American males in stores because we believe they are thieves, then they become the "usual suspect" when something is missing in the classroom. Also, as in the larger society, when the African American male steps outside of his prescribed role, when the African American student asserts his manhood and defends his integrity, he is severely punished.

When teachers are more comfortable with the Sambo image of African American male students, they relate better to the jovial, playful African American male than the serious, quiet one who is perceived to have an "attitude." The Sambo image also creates greater acceptance for the African American male student who is submissive rather than assertive, the latter being perceived as aggressive or defiant (Bireda, 2000).

When teachers see the African American male as the Brute, they respond to him with fear; they are afraid to admonish him or to wake him when he sleeps in class. The Brute image leads to a preoccupation with control and unjust labeling. He is punished most often for minor offenses (Bireda, 2000).

INEQUALITIES IN DISCIPLINARY PRACTICES

Inequities and disparities in disciplinary practices result from cultural misunderstandings and unconscious stereotyping due to cultural conditioning. Described below are ten consequences of cultural conflicts and stereotyping in the classroom.

Unrealistic Expectations

We tend to hold African American students to much higher standards of behavior than we do other groups of students. In fact, developmental norms are literally "thrown out of the window" when it comes to African American students, especially males. We never allow African American males, in particular, the luxury of "being boys." They are routinely more harshly punished for misbehavior that is considered normal for youngsters.

These unrealistic expectations begin in kindergarten when young males with high energy levels (like most healthy boys their age) don't sit still and are labeled hyperactive. When young African Americans get off the bus, in many instances after long bus rides, they are expected (in the words of one African American teacher) "to walk like little soldiers" to the building. African American adolescents like others their age, are ruled more by hormones than clear thinking.

Much of the "misbehavior" for which African American males in particular are punished severely is typical of youth their age. From the first day of school, the control of African American males begins. They are punished more often and more severely for the typical misbehavior of children and youth their ages.

Faulty Assumptions

On many occasions, teachers are very quick to assume that a misdeed is intended on the part of the African American male, when his actions are really quite innocent. The stereotype of the oversexed Black male looms just beneath the surface. The following two examples of this involve very young African American males.

In one instance, a young male had been given a pair of 3-D glasses. He had spent the evening pretending to see through plants, walls, clothing, and the like. The next day he took the glasses to school (which he should not have been allowed to do). He told a Caucasian classmate, "I can see through your clothes." The teacher overheard the comment and referred the student to the office for "sexually inappropriate behavior." The parents were livid and explained that there was no sexual intent in his statement; he merely meant that his 3-D glasses could penetrate all types of surfaces, including clothing.

In another case, a young African American boy went to the bathroom, forgot to zip his pants, and came out. One of his Caucasian female classmates told the teacher, who then referred the young boy to the office for "sexual harassment." His parents could not understand why the teacher could not have simply told their son to zip his pants.

On occasion, Caucasian female teachers have spoken of African American males "exuding sexuality" or sensing a type of "sexual come-on" on the part of African American males, which produces a type of "sexual tension" between them and the student that they find uncomfortable.

Faulty assumptions especially about the "innate badness" of poor African American children often deny them the opportunity to receive badly needed support services. As I have interviewed and worked with African American students who were frequently suspended from school, I discovered that many of them were experiencing severe personal and family problems.

Some are having the typical disagreements with parents; others are experiencing deep resentment of an absent father. One student in particular who was repeatedly in trouble and suspended was in great need of grief counseling as he had gone home from school to discover his deceased mother. Many other students who were repeatedly suspended from school were obviously depressed. When faulty assumptions are made about students, punishment is the first course of action and their need for counseling or other intervention is neglected.

Behavior Tracking

In the same way that African American students are tracked academically, they are tracked behaviorally. First of all, we expect him to misbehave, and when he does, he enters a track that he cannot escape. He will never start another day "tabula rasa"; he is tarnished. He will get no breaks and no second chances because once he misbehaves, he wears a label.

I once observed in a classroom where the teacher pulled out a file that she kept on one African American male student in particular. She said that one of the first things she did each day was to date a sheet of paper and wait for him to misbehave because she knew he would.

The result of behavior tracking comes in the words of an African American mother who was distressed because her son had dropped out of school. She begged him not too, but he said that he could not take it anymore because "they won't let me change." Another student commented, "I am trying to change, but it seems like its no use. Sometime, I don't even want to come back."

Inconsistency

One of the complaints heard most often from African American males and their parents is that discipline is inconsistent; in their words, "there are different rules for different students." Many of the complaints of racism come from the student's perception that non–African American and middle-class students are not punished or are not punished as severely as are African American males. African American students are very much aware of any inconsistencies and are always watching to see if a teacher is going to be fair in administering consequences for misbehavior.

African American parents tell me that they want their children punished when they misbehave, but that they want the same rules that apply for their children to apply to all others. In a workshop, a teacher told of how he had come to a level of greater awareness with regard to consistency in discipline.

He had admonished two African American students for their behavior and said that the next person to make a sound is "out of here." Well, the next person to make a sound was a Caucasian male student who simply said "e." At that moment, the teacher said that he saw and felt the eyes of every African American student in that room; they were all waiting to see if he would be true to his word and send the Caucasian out of the classroom. He said that until that day, he never knew the extent to which African American students observed their teachers to see if they were consistent in applying the rules.

Students who attend predominately African American schools report favoritism based on student grades or attitudes. They feel that some students get away with a lot while others are "targeted." One young man stated," I see others doing things; if it were me, I would get the worse consequences."

Leading Behaviors

In many cases, African American males are "set up" for misbehavior. The teacher knows which "button to push" so that the student "goes off" or becomes verbally abusive. I have been told by teachers that this is a technique that is often used by some teachers when they do not wish to have a student in their class on a particular day or any day.

In this case, the teacher simply says whatever he or she knows will upset the student to the point that he reacts and is subsequently sent to the office. Lacking maturity, these students never seem to understand that this is a ploy. African American male students have complained to me, however, that often they "feel like they are in a constant battle."

Teacher provocation is the one behavior that African American males most report. Below are just some of the comments that express their feelings about teacher actions in this regard:

- "I can tell she doesn't want me in the class. She wants me to withdraw. She keeps coming at me; eventually I break down and get kicked out."
- "If you ask a question, she looks at you like you are a fool; it makes you want to say something to her, tell her about herself."

- "Our conflict began on the first day of school when I pulled my shirt out before I left the building. Since then, he has been trying to provoke me. Little slick things; the least little thing to get me out of class."

Finally, I observed the following interaction in a classroom. These comments were made to one student in the span of a few minutes.

- "Fix your clothes." (He tucked his shirt in.)
- "Get your feet off the back of the chair." (He did.)
- Stop calling out the answer." (Student had been raising his hand but was ignored.)
- " Open your eyes." (He replied, "my eyes ain't closed.")
- She corrected his speech.

Personal Disregard

Because African American students are expected to be lazy and irresponsible, to not care about their schoolwork or getting an education, in some ways, they become invisible. They often complain that they are ignored and not listened to. Most often, they complain of being disrespected. Many times, they feel that they are not listened to or respected until they "go off." In the last chapter, I talked about the sensitivity of the African American male to what he perceives to be disrespect. Below are some feelings expressed by African American males about what they consider to be disrespect.

- Student was wearing a tee shirt (yellow) of a prohibited color underneath his outer uniform shirt. "She tried to embarrass me in front of everyone. Why did she have to yell at me? She could have just asked me to button up."
- "My teacher is just rude." He recounts these two incidents: When a student didn't have paper, teacher says: "If you can buy designer clothes, you can buy paper."
  When students were allowed to share snacks, teacher says to one student: "We don't want any of that food stamp food."
- "She interrupts me, won't listen to me. She gets 30 minutes, [to make her point] and I get two seconds."
- "At least listen to me, let me explain. It didn't happen like that."
- "I snap when I feel disrespected, yelled at, just talk to me."
- "Talk to me with respect; it makes me angry, we are both human. Pull me to the side."

There is the belief that African American students only respond to harsh treatment; that they don't understand anything else. There is a difference between firm, harsh, and disrespectful behavior toward a student. If a student comes from a home background where harshness is the norm, that is even more reason to teach him a better way of interacting with others.

Failure to Take Advantage of Teachable Moments

Discipline involves both punishment and teaching. The focus of most disciplinary action with African American males is punishment. African American parents often ask why the school official didn't talk to their son and explain to him why what he did was wrong. An African American parent volunteer in the school bookstore observed the way in which two incidents involving the theft of a pencil from the bookstore were handled by a teacher.

In the first instance, an African American male stole a pencil and was immediately referred to the office for ISS (in-school suspension). In the next instance, involving the same teacher, a Caucasian male stole a pencil. However, rather than being referred to the office, he was given a lecture on why it was wrong to steal. The volunteer felt that it was assumed that African Americans would steal and the little boy had to be "taught a lesson," while the stealing on the part of the non–African American student was considered to be a less serious matter.

There are other times when teaching is the most effective approach. An African American high school student referred to one of his favorite teachers as "his dog" and was overheard by an administrator. The administrator became very angry and admonished the student to never use that term again. The student was very confused and felt embarrassed and put down by the administrator.

A much better way to have handled the situation would have been to make this a "teachable moment" and explain to the student that some terms, although appropriate to use when referring to and communicating with one's peers, are considered inappropriate in the school setting. In this way, the student would have learned a valuable lesson without undermining his self-esteem.

Failure to Acknowledge and Respect Cultural Differences

Stereotypes get in the way of acknowledging and respecting cultural differences. When one's beliefs about African American males are based upon negative stereotypical images, it is more difficult to view differences as differences rather than deficits.

Excessive noise is often an offense for which African American males are referred. In these cases, the African American male will be viewed as loud and emotional because he is considered to be uncouth and untrained. Often his failure to establish direct eye contact will be considered to be a sure indicator of his dishonesty.

Excessive Punishment

A common complaint of African American parents is that the punishment often far exceeds the offense. There appears to be a belief that because of innate character deficits and a proclivity for thievery, fighting, and disruptive behavior, African American males who break the rules should be "made examples of," to warn all others that this behavior will not be tolerated.

In one case, an elementary school student who was "clowning around" in the cafeteria was publicly paddled over the school intercom. In another instance following Halloween, a high school teacher allowed his class to eat candy in class. An African American male threw the stick from a lollipop out of the window. The student was told to do 100 push-ups and warned that if he stopped he would be made to start over. The student said that he would not do 100 push-ups because he physically could not do 100 push-ups (he was very slight in build). The student was referred for insubordination.

Some punishment serves no real purpose, in that it does not correct behavior; for instance when students in some cases are rewarded for cutting class or being tardy by being suspended. One student who had excessive tardies, 22 to be exact, was suspended for one day; he was suspended another two days for missing his fourth block class; then ultimately ended up with five days out-of-school suspensions for cutting class on two other occasions.

Repeated behaviors such as tardiness or cutting class are symptomatic of deeper problems, indicating that intervention is needed. Allowing a student to have one and two- day vacations from school does nothing to address the problem and more significantly contributes to the academic/discipline cycle of failure.

Finally, the criminalization of student misbehavior is rampant, especially in predominately African American schools. Students who fight are arrested and those who witness and do not report a fight are often suspended as well.

Intolerance for Violation of "Group Assigned" Behaviors

The purpose of stereotyping is to control the targeted group, so stereotypes are always accompanied by a code or set of rules by which the victim of the stereotype must abide. These rules regulate the personal behavior of the targeted group.

There has always been a written and unwritten code of behavior for African American males that, like the stereotypes themselves, has been transmitted from generation to generation. Like stereotypes, these codes operate at an unconscious level; without our awareness, they can influence our reactions to certain behaviors in African American males. When African American males violate this historical code, they are usually severely punished.

Below are five of the major historical or Black codes that governed the behavior of African American males, and the interpretation of the violations of these codes in the modern-day school setting.

Three or More Black Males Shall Not Gather

It was originally felt that if Blacks were allowed to congregate, they might conspire against the enslavers. The sight of Black men gathering created fear in Whites. Today, the sight of three or more African American males still produces fear. Oftentimes, African American males walking down the hall or sitting together in the cafeteria can create feelings of uneasiness.

Never Strike a White

African Americans have always been severely punished for striking Whites. African American parents often complain that their son was punished more severely when he was involved in a fight with a White student. In many cases, the African American male is punished for starting a fight when he strikes a White student for using the "n" word. Most often, the White student remains unpunished for the use of the "n" word; what happens, in effect, is that the original victim of racial harassment and verbal assault now becomes the perpetrator of the offense.

Never Raise Your Voice at a White

When the African American male becomes emotional, his behavior is considered to be verbally aggressive or disruptive. In many cases, his volume increases when he is attempting to state his case or defend himself.

Never Contradict a White

When African American males feel that they are being treated unfairly, they will insist on "being heard." This behavior usually gets them into trouble and the student is labeled argumentative, insubordinate, or defiant.

Be Submissive

When African American males are not submissive in speech or manner, they risk the danger of getting into real difficulty. They are assumed to have an "attitude." This lack of submission is usually met with a show of power with the intention of showing them who is in control. Even African American males who are excellent students get into trouble when they do not display humility or act "too proud." This "attitude" is what seems to be most offensive to many teachers and administrators.

A middle-class African American teacher recalled how her two sons were treated very differently in the school setting. The oldest one, the smarter of the two, is very serious, doesn't joke or play around, and is considered by his teachers to have an attitude. His younger brother, who is not as bright academically, is more outgoing and jovial. He is considered an ideal student and has never had a discipline problem. The mother of these two students is certain that her elder son's lack of submissiveness is what causes problems for him at school.

The belief that the African American male must be controlled is based on the historical image of the Brute. The need to exercise control and to demonstrate authority is one of the major causes of tension, conflict, and disciplinary problems involving the African American male student.

When a "show of power" is used unnecessarily, it will provoke a negative reaction in the African American male student. He will most definitely strike back when he feels that he is challenged, humiliated, ignored, or treated unfairly. This, of course, creates a "lose–lose" situation in the classroom. The African American male student will most definitely lose because he will face some type of disciplinary action. The teacher also loses, however, because students are always watching, and they will lose respect for the teacher who must exercise power in this manner.

African American students, in epidemic proportions, are being trapped in a cycle that leads to disciplinary referrals, detention, in-school suspension, expulsion, or placement in an alternative setting. This cycle ultimately ends with academic failure and dropping out. For many, the future beckons even more bleak: incarceration is the last stop in the cycle.

The belief that African American students and males in particular must be controlled gets at the heart of the matter of racial disparity in discipline as relates to these students. The school culture and climate determines what the experience of the African American student will be in an either a predominately mainstream or predominately ethnic minority school.

In the next chapter, we will examine the school climate and the ways in which it can contribute to disciplinary events.

RECOMMENDATIONS

Do: When you write a referral, determine if the referral is in any way, the result of:

- Misperceptions
- The projection of stereotypes
- Inappropriate expectations

Chapter 8

School Discipline and School Climate

The goal of school discipline is to create school environments that are safe and orderly so that teachers can teach and students can learn. Some school environments, however, actually work against this goal in that they promote and perpetuate discipline events. Research indicates that positive perceptions of a school's racial climate are associated with both higher student achievement and fewer discipline problems (Mattison and Abner, 2007). In this chapter, we will examine the types of school climates that promote and perpetuate rather than lessen the number of discipline events that occur.

First of all, it is important to remember that the school experiences of students from caste/involuntary minority groups mirror those of their parents and other adults of their group in mainstream society. If African American men are feared and profiled in the larger society, then African American male students will have the same experience in the school setting. Our schools like other institutions mirror American society in general.

Two factors—the *school culture,* and *school climate*—determine the quality of the school experiences of students from caste/involuntary minority groups. The *school culture* (i.e., the beliefs, values, and assumptions that guide school policies and practices) shapes the *school climate* (i.e., atmosphere or feel of the school). If the ideology of inferiority (intellectual and cultural) undergirds the belief structure about students from caste/involuntary minority groups,then policies and practices will reflect this ideology, resulting in a school climate that is not inviting and ,in some cases, is even hostile to students from caste/involuntary minority groups.

A school's culture and climate not only can support or impede the learning process of students from caste/involuntary minority groups but also determines the discipline policies and practices as it relates to these students.

The school culture and climate will influence how "discipline is experienced" by students from caste/involuntary minority groups. The school climate can, to a large extent, even impact student behavior, especially when it serves as a catalyst for student resentment, rebelliousness, and ultimate acting out.

The lack of understanding of the culture of African American students and culturally conditioned beliefs about African Americans, especially males, makes control the goal of discipline for African American students. This control through discipline policies and practices is applied to African American students in both predominately mainstream and predominately African American schools but may be experienced by the students in different ways.

In both cases, however, these discipline practices elicit anger, resentment, and rebelliousness from African American students. Much of the behavior described as "defiance" is a reaction to the powerlessness felt by African American students in these school environments.

PREDOMINATELY MAINSTREAM SCHOOLS

In terms of discipline, African American students often experience school climates as hostile. Discipline for African American students is dispensed arbitrarily, swiftly, harshly, and unfairly.

African American students most often describe feelings of being targeted, of being repeatedly sent out of class for doing little or nothing. African American students also reported feelings of being constantly under surveillance: "she keeps her eyes on us."

What is most disheartening to hear from these students is their sense of powerlessness: "they won't listen to us, we are always wrong." Most often, it is due to this sense of powerlessness, the feeling of being disrespected, and their need to defend themselves in an environment in which one student described as "feeling like and outcast," that leads to discipline events and suspensions.

PREDOMINATELY ETHNIC MINORITY SCHOOLS

There is the unfounded and misguided belief that unfair discipline practices are only a problem in predominately mainstream schools. It is assumed that for instance, since the majority of the students are African American that the culture of these students is respected and that stereotyping does not occur. Nothing could be farther from the truth. Unwarranted and excessive discipline is a major problem in predominately ethnic minority schools. In view of the numbers of low achieving predominately ethnic minority schools, it is imperative that we examine more closely the discipline policies and practices in these schools.

The very same school-related factors that result in large numbers of African American students being suspended from predominately mainstream schools are operative in predominately African American schools. As was stated earlier, predominately African American and Hispanic/Latino schools are most likely to have zero-tolerance policies. The climate of many predominately African American schools is very authoritarian and punitive. At some level, conscious or unconscious, it is believed that the large numbers of minority and poor students makes the need for such an approach to discipline absolutely necessary.

In many predominately African American schools, the attempt to control all aspects of student life and behavior is pervasive. Students describe this type of climate as "feeling like a jail." Their feelings are probably warranted in that jail terminology or jargon is part of the school lexicon; one hears of "holding cells" (where large groups of students are sequestered), "lockdown", "death row" (a row in which all males are seated), and "repeat offender" (students who have been suspended many times).

In an extreme case, student movement is constantly monitored (i.e., not being able to go to the bathroom during the first or last 30 minutes of a 90-minute block class); dress codes are rigidly enforced (i.e., students being referred for a shirt untucked, not wearing a belt, or forgetting to wear an identification badge). In this type of school climate, a general feeling of tension exists with both teachers and students expressing feelings of "we vs. them" and being in "separate camps."

For African American students, a most unfortunate consequence of this type of school environment is the lack of outlets for student involvement and leadership development. Students report that they are not allowed to engage in group work because" they are afraid that we might get out of control."

As with African American students in predominately mainstream schools, students in predominately African American schools also feel disrespected and not listened to. The students that I have interviewed and worked with express feelings of deep resentment about not being trusted and being controlled.

The type of atmosphere described above does not promote a positive learning environment, in fact it in many ways incites student misbehavior. The level of powerlessness produced only encourages student rebellion in the form of disobeying rules, disrespect, and defiance. This type of school climate invites rather than lessens the number of discipline events. The authoritarian-punitive-control oriented schools that focus on obedience and subservience are an expression of the historical Black codes that were used to govern the movement and behavior of African Americans, especially males.

The goal of this book is to help readers understand the school-related factors and dynamics which result in unfair discipline practices as a way of decreasing not only the number of suspensions but discipline events as well. Whether it is a predominately mainstream or predominately ethnic minority school, decreasing and preventing the occurrence of discipline events will require a change in the school culture and climate.

The principal plays a primary role in this process. He or she provides the leadership, articulates goals and behavioral expectations of teachers, and provides professional development and support during the process. In the next chapter, we will more fully examine the principal's role in guiding the process of changing the school climate.

RECOMMENDATIONS

Do: Initiate a dialogue with African American students.

- Discuss perceptions of the school climate.
- Discuss feelings about the way discipline is dispensed.
- Use student input in helping to design fair and effective discipline practices.

Part III

Chapter 9

Changing the School Climate
The Administrator's Role

Eliminating school-related factors that place African American students at greater risk for disciplinary referrals and actions requires that fundamental and significant changes occur in the school culture and environment. Two types of changes on two different levels must take place. Changes related to culturally responsive and culturally responsible actions must occur at both the institutional and individual levels.

Culturally responsive actions include those social practices that acknowledge and respect cultural differences, especially those differences that occur in communication patterns and styles. This change is based upon the recognition that a student's identity is shaped by his culture and that cultural connectivity is essential for his healthy functioning and growth. To require an African American student to deny his culture is to require him to deny a core part of himself.

From my many years of experience as a codependency counselor, I know that the denial of the self is very destructive to the individual; this type of denial produces a marginalized rather than a healthy individual. Also, it is important to remember that the ultimate attempt to control or dehumanize enslaved African people was to try to destroy their cultural identity and deny them cultural expression. We do not want to repeat this type of culturally destructive behavior in our school settings.

Respecting the African American student's cultural identity does not mean that we don't have rules and regulations. It does mean, however, that we recognize that in a diverse society, in schools with culturally diverse student populations, the policies and regulations that we establish must neither give privilege to any particular group nor penalize any group because of cultural differences.

At the institutional or school level, changes that relate to cultural responsiveness involve a revision of policies and procedures that are discriminatory and leave room for abuse. It also includes a system of teacher accountability and evaluation that emphasizes the teacher's ability to demonstrate culturally sensitive and responsive behaviors toward all students.

At the individual level, cultural responsiveness involves honestly assessing one's beliefs about African American students, and one's interactions with them. It also involves the practice of cultural etiquette. To create a school environment in which culturally responsive and culturally responsible behavior is the norm requires courageous leadership on the part of the principal, and a commitment to the process by the faculty and staff.

In this chapter, I discuss the principal's role in changing the school climate, and the process that must be undertaken if a school is serious about reducing the disciplinary problems encountered by African American students.

THE PRINCIPAL'S ROLE

From my work in schools, I have come to believe that the principal's attitude and commitment to creating a culturally sensitive school environment is the most important element in bringing about the needed changes. The principal must set the tone, initiate the process, guide the process, and hold teachers accountable for creating a classroom environment in which all students feel respected and are treated fairly. The role of the principal is to provide the leadership necessary to create a school environment that is characterized by both culturally responsive and culturally responsible behaviors toward students. Ultimately, the principal has the responsibility for ensuring the elimination of any school-related factors that place African American students at risk for disciplinary referrals.

In order to create this culturally sensitive school environment, the principal must give attention to the outcomes of specific groups of students, especially those students who are most at risk of experiencing difficulties in the school setting and becoming non-completers—generally, poor African American males.

The principal must model culturally responsive and responsible behaviors, provide needed information to increase teacher competency, and coach those teachers who are uncomfortable or resistant to the process. Finally, the principal must set the standards for professional ethics and establish the criteria for evaluation as it pertains to cultural sensitivity in the specific school environment.

The principal must provide leadership in three key areas: (1) initiating the process, (2) guiding the process, and (3) evaluating the process. In this chapter, I provide strategies for initiating and guiding the process. In Chapter 12, I discuss evaluating the effectiveness of the process in creating a school environment that is sensitive and responsive to the culture and experiences of African American students.

INITIATING THE CHANGE PROCESS

In the initiation phase of the process, the principal must determine the faculty's

- Attitudes toward African American students
- Perceptions of the need to specifically address issues related to African American male students
- Openness to participate in the process
- Level of support that is needed to make the process successful
- Sense of buy-in or ownership of the process

Step 1: Assessing Faculty Attitudes toward African American Students

The attitudes held toward African American students by faculty members will, to a large extent, determine the faculty's perception of the need to examine school-related factors that may lead to disparities in the disciplinary process. The first task of the principal, therefore, is to make some determination about the attitudes held toward African American students.

This can be done in two ways: by conducting an informal climate audit and through dialogues with faculty members. Since beliefs precede behaviors, the best way to get a feel for teacher attitudes toward African American students is to observe interactions between teachers and students in classrooms and other campus settings. The purpose of the observations and the dialogues is to help the principal determine the beliefs that are held about, and the feelings toward, African American students.

At this point, the principal should also be interested in determining the extent to which faculty members understand or feel that they understand the culture of African American students. Finally, it is important to see the type and quality of interactions between African American students and their teachers.

A point of departure for the dialogues may simply be "We seem to be experiencing a number of disciplinary problems with our African American male students. What do you feel is the cause of these problems?" It is important at this point for the principal to create a climate in which faculty members feel free to express their beliefs and feelings toward the students.

To eliminate the school-related at-risk factors for African American students, changes will have to occur in the faculty's (1) belief system regarding African American, (2) feelings toward African Americans, (3) level of knowledge about the culture of African Americans, and (4) interactions with and behaviors toward African American students.

Step 2: Establishing the Need for Change

As I was in the process of completing this book, I received a call from an administrator who was interested in my working with her faculty on issues related to African American males. Like many schools, they had a disproportionate number of African American males who were referred for, and were the recipients of, disciplinary actions.

The principal was concerned, however, about resistance from the faculty. It seemed that several faculty members were complaining that the focus of the training was on African American males. It was their feeling that they should be concerned about all of the students rather than focusing on this group. In this case, the principal would have to establish or indicate the need to focus on this particular group of students.

To help establish a need, today's principal has to rely on statistical data, disaggregated by race, gender, and social class, if possible. By using this type of data, a picture will emerge that clearly shows the group of students that presents the most critical need for attention. Given that all faculty members are interested in preventing and decreasing the number of discipline problems rather than merely punishing the students who commit offenses, the principal must determine the root causes of the problem.

Conducting separate focus groups with teachers, students, and parents can provide insights that will support the need to focus on the issues related to African American students and discipline. At one parent forum that focused only on the issue of discipline, sixty-five African American parents attended. School officials were amazed because they had previously had little success in getting African American parents to attend meetings. The attendance of these parents decried the myth that African American parents do not care about their children's education.

These parents were very concerned about what was happening to their children, and disparity in discipline was a major concern. Also, to the surprise of the school officials, these African American parents did want their children disciplined. They, however, wanted discipline to be administered in a fair and consistent manner. In one of the districts in which I work, the superintendent's attitude is that "If there is a perception of a problem, then there is a problem." African American parents are starting to voice many concerns, and to seek redress in the courts for issues related to disparities in discipline.

Although many faculty members may not be as inclined to hear the opinions of students regarding why they misbehave, and the disciplinary process in general, I do recommend that input be solicited from students as well. It is important to hear from the students who are experiencing the most problems in the area of discipline. It was after hearing the feelings of students, especially those who were frequently in trouble that I decided to look into and address the school-related issues.

Step 3: Motivating the Faculty to Be Open to the Process

In order to reduce disproportionality in disciplinary referrals and to eliminate school-related factors that contribute to the problem, the faculty must be willing to participate in the process. A combination of the "stick and carrot" approach appears to be the most effective.

The "carrot" in learning how to better understand and relate to African American students is that it will simply make life easier for the teacher. Cross-cultural interactions can be very stressful if one does not understand or appreciate cultural differences. Holding stereotypes, even unconscious ones, produces stress in the form of fear and the feeling that one has to constantly maintain some sense of control when interacting with the stereotyped individual.

Adopting culturally responsive and responsible behaviors will reduce teacher stress, promote better relationships with African American students, and add to teaching effectiveness. From a basically selfish point of view, teaching African American students will become infinitely easier if the teacher actively engages in this process.

From the point of view of teacher accountability and professional standards, teachers have an ethical responsibility to learn how to effectively teach all students well. Teaching today is not like it was when I started teaching in the 1960s. Most of us teach students who come from cultural backgrounds very different from our own. Some of us teach students that we never thought we would teach, and unfortunately, through the process of cultural conditioning, may have negative views of and hold low expectations for those students.

Teaching a diverse student population is the new reality; these are our customers, these are the students that we are ethically bound to teach in the best way that we can. Learning accurate information and unlearning erroneous beliefs is part of our responsibility as professional teachers; it is also the key to our professional empowerment.

Once, in a workshop, as I talked about the new student population, the new challenges, and the new paradigms that we as teachers would have to adapt to, a teacher bemoaned this new teaching reality, and wondered out loud, "Why can't things just be the way they were fifty years ago?" Well, unfortunately or fortunately, things are not, and will never be, the way they were fifty years ago.

The new teaching reality requires that teacher evaluations and promotions consider culturally responsive and responsible behavior as part of the evaluation criteria. The principal must in no uncertain terms make it clear that in this school environment, teacher effectiveness includes the willingness to grow as a teacher (actively participate in the change process) and the demonstration of culturally responsive and responsible behaviors.

Step 4: Support the Development of New Competencies

Professional development in the form of training related to African American culture, African American male identity issues, and dealing with stereotypes must be provided for the faculty. The lack of accurate information about African American culture and African American males is a major contributor to the problems that occur between African American male students and their teachers. This professional development should not be limited to a day or two of training, but should include the opportunity for teachers to engage in ongoing dialogue about the issues.

Instituting a buddy system, matching teachers who have problems with teachers who are most effective in teaching African American students and who have few discipline problems with these students, can be very beneficial. There is always at least one teacher who can establish a relationship with the most troubled student. Have the teachers who are experiencing the most problems (the most referrals) seek advice from and observe the more effective teachers.

It is important for the principal to emphasize throughout the process that this is not intended as teacher bashing; it is a way to help teachers find ways to be more effective in reducing tension and conflict between themselves and African American students.

Step 5: Promoting Ownership of the Process

This process is intended to change the school culture. As such, it requires not only the active participation of the faculty, but also their "buy-in" and ownership of the process. Reducing disciplinary referrals and actions among African American male students must be a school goal.

Eliminating the school-related factors that contribute to these disciplinary referrals and actions must also be a school goal. It is imperative that this process become a school-wide project, with a plan developed to systematically bring about change. Although the principal has the responsibility of initiating and guiding the process, all members of the school community must be included in the process: teachers, students, parents, and interested community leaders.

ENSURING EQUITY THROUGH CHANGES IN POLICIES AND PROCEDURES

Eliminating school-related factors that lead to disparities in the disciplinary process require that changes occur at the policy-and-procedure level. This process will be initiated by the principal and implemented through the involvement of teachers, parents, students, and individuals from the community.

Below are suggested ways to make changes in policies and procedures that will promote culturally responsive and responsible behaviors related to the issue of discipline.

1. Form a committee made up of teachers, students, parents, and community members to review the current student disciplinary policies and procedures.
2. Make revisions in policies where necessary to ensure that there is no possibility for vague interpretations, abuse, or disparate treatment.
3. Clearly define the criteria for offense categories. What is considered disruptive, disrespectful, defiant, argumentative, or verbally aggressive behavior depends a great deal on subjective or individual interpretation. Try to come to some clear and consistent interpretation that leaves little room for unfairness.
4. Base assessment of punishment on objective criteria. Leave no room for excessive or retaliatory punishment.
5. Clearly define how disciplinary sanctions will be imposed for specific offenses.
6. Make the examination of precipitating factors or events a part of the disciplinary process. It is important to rule out any instance of harassing or provocative behavior on the part of the teacher.
7. Allow input from a number of individuals prior to the imposition of serious sanctions (long-term suspensions, expulsions, or placement in an alternative school setting).

8. Any deviations from the established student disciplinary policies and procedures must be documented and approved by the committee that reviewed student disciplinary policies.
9. Establish policies and disciplinary penalties for racial harassment if none are in place.
10. Implement a procedure for providing conflict resolution training for teachers, and establish criteria for the participation of the teacher and student in the conflict resolution process.
11. Establish a procedure for assisting teachers who make an excessive amount of referrals for offenses that could be handled in the classroom.
12. Establish a procedure for investigating allegations of racism, classism, and other abuses of power.

Two additional changes must occur if school-related risk factors are to be eliminated. First, the importance of establishing good teacher–student relationships must be emphasized. The quality of the teacher–student relationship will determine the effectiveness of that interaction. It is also important to remember that African American students are socialized in a collective culture. Social relationships are important and that includes the student's relationship with his teacher. When teachers have good relationships with African American students, discipline is less of a problem.

Second, the stated and unstated emphasis in the school setting must be on academics rather than discipline. There is a distinctive difference in the feel of schools whose focus is academics versus those schools whose focus is control and discipline. In many cases, schools with a predominately African American or low-income student population emphasize discipline rather than academics.

For example, in schools that I have visited with a predominately minority and lower-income student population, I saw more information on bulletin boards relating to following the rules and building acceptable character. On the other hand, bulletin boards in the schools that emphasized academics were devoted to content areas of the curriculum and providing new information.

For some reason, it appears at least from the informal curriculum in many schools that I visit, minority, especially poor African American students, spend more time in improving their character and learning to follow rules than focusing on academics. It is ironic, however, that in schools where the emphasis is on good teaching, with high expectations for student success, discipline tends to be less of an issue.

The process of better understanding the African American student and of transcending stereotypes begins with the individual. In the next chapter, we discuss ways in which to change individual attitudes.

RECOMMENDATIONS

Do: Initiate the change process in your school.

- Determine what changes are necessary to make your school environment more culturally responsive and responsible.
- Determine what role each individual and team will play.

Chapter 10

Changing Individual Attitudes

At the heart of the matter is a simple equation balancing the relationship that exists between the African American student, his culture, and his teacher. The quality of that relationship will determine if communication and rapport, or tension and conflict, occurs between them.

A lack of knowledge and understanding of the culture of African American students will interfere with the creation of effective communication between the teacher and student. Faulty assumptions, erroneous beliefs, and fear that result from historical stereotypes will block the development of a healthy relationship between teacher and student.

Changes in the school climate can only come about if changes occur at the individual level. The will to be more effective in establishing rapport, communicating, and developing relationships with African American students is essential.

Some years ago, I assisted a Superintendent's Advisory Committee in developing a Cultural Awareness Guide for all current and incoming teachers at one of the schools in which I worked. One of the major issues that the district was addressing was racial disparity in discipline.

Tables 10.1 and 10.2 were developed by the Discipline and Classroom Management Writing Team. These exercises are for you, the reader. Reflect and answer the questions on the self-evaluation as honestly as possible. Don't be afraid of seeing areas in which you need to improve or develop; a conscious awareness of your relationship issues with African American students is key to correcting these issues and decreasing conflicts with them. The Do's and Don'ts presented in Table 10.2 are excellent techniques for decreasing tension, conflicts, and discipline referrals.

79

Table 10.1. Self-Evaluation

Directions: Please read and answer honestly. No one will see this but you.

Question	Yes/No
1. Have you had an excessive number of discipline referrals in the past?	_____
2. Do you bring personal issues into the classroom?	_____
3. Do you tend to have excessive referrals on a particular student?	_____
4. Do you tend to demand eye contact from students?	_____
5. Do you have your classroom rules posted and stated clearly?	_____
6. Do you utilize the services of the school counselor?	_____
7. Do you utilize the suggestions of the school counselor once you have referred a student?	_____
8. Do you show your students respect?	_____
9. Is your classroom structured to ensure that students are actively engaged in learning?	_____
10. Do you encourage student interaction among diverse cultural groups (for example, seating arrangements and cooperative groups)?	_____
11. Do you set high expectations for ALL students?	_____
12. Do you discuss former students with other teachers in a negative way?	_____
13. Do you have any preconceived notions about a particular group of students?	_____
14. Do you hold grudges against students?	_____
15. Do you punish students excessively?	_____

Four broad categories of strategies are helpful to the teacher and administrator in developing attitudes and behaviors that will enhance the relationship between him or her and the African American students.

First, acquiring accurate information about the cultural attributes of African American students, acknowledging and appreciating the differences between African American and European-based mainstream culture, and practicing the cultural etiquette described in Chapter 5 are a starting point.

Secondly, two instruments designed by the Superintendent's Advisory Committee can be very beneficial in assessing relationships with students, and in providing culturally effective classroom management strategies (see Tables 10.1 and 10.2).

Third, following two basic rules related to making referrals that stem from inappropriate student behavior can help you make the most effective type of referral to change student behavior. Finally, engage in a cognitive restructuring process to identify, challenge, and change erroneous beliefs based upon culturally conditioned myths and stereotypes.

Table 10.2. Culturally Effective/Ineffective Classroom Management Techniques

DO	DON'T
allow student to have time out after disciplinary action has been taken	have too many rules
allow students point of view to be heard	get in the face of a student (sign of aggression)
use "teachable moments"	yell
keep your "cool"	demand eye contact
post reasonable rules	touch (in a situation with anger)
refer problem students to counselor	demand student to use "Yes, Ma'am" or "Yes, Sir"
be willing to try counselor's strategies	call students "boy" or "girl"
be aware of your own baggage (for example, having a bad day or argument with spouse)	make situations a power struggle deny students their right to be heard
be consistent	take it personally
realize you are not perfect	expect submissiveness (threatening)
be willing to say you are sorry expect respect for authority	allow/encourage hearsay (mutual respect)

WHAT, WHEN, AND WHERE TO REFER

"Seasoned" teachers have expressed with pride to me that they make few referrals to the office because "I can handle my problems myself in the classroom." One reason that "they take care of their own problems" is that they feel it is part of "good teaching." Secondly, they do not want to convey the message to the student that they are unable to handle them. Thirdly, they will say that they have learned from experience that whoever disciplines the student is the adult who earns the student's respect, and they refuse to give away their power.

One aspect of good classroom management is learning what, when, and where to refer students when inappropriate behavior occurs in the classroom. Two guidelines that teachers with good classroom management follow are

1. Remember that all human behavior is goal-directed; there is some need that the student who is acting out is trying to meet. Ask yourself: "Why is this student acting-out? Why is this student frustrated in this class?"
2. A referral should always assist the student in some way to change his or her behavior; therefore, even discipline should be more than simply punishment. In an educational setting, there must be an educational component as well. Ask yourself: "How will this referral help the student to change his or her behavior?"

Glasser (1986) posits that still another question be asked: "What can the teacher do to help the disruptive student to find the class more satisfying?" He suggests that only a discipline program that is also concerned with classroom satisfaction will work.

"Exceptional" teachers, counselors, and social workers who are also peer facilitators described student behaviors in terms of four categories of teacher responses: (1) incidents to ignore, (2) incidents in which the teacher would take advantage of a "teachable moment," (3) incidents that provided the teacher an opportunity to examine his classroom management style, and (4) incidents that required a referral of some type. The referrals were of six types: (1) counselor, (2) parent, (3) peer, (4) student support team, (5) adult mentor, and (6) administrator.

The facilitators felt that some incidents did not warrant giving the student the power to draw attention away from teaching the class; if the behavior persisted, and was truly disruptive for the class, then it would be dealt with. They felt that teaching is part of disciplining, and that some incidents would not occur again or would lessen if students were taught why they were inappropriate. The teachers also felt that some number of incidents could be prevented if the teacher used more effective classroom management skills. As you will see in table 10-3, these "exceptional" and "seasoned" teachers referred only the most serious offenses to an administrator.

GIVING UP THE NEED TO CONTROL

The one thing that was central to the discipline practices of these teachers-facilitators was that they had no sense of a need to "control" their students. They believed that they should focus on "good teaching"—challenging, hands-on activities to keep students involved so that they didn't have time for excesses, cooperative learning and peer tutoring that allowed "structured socialization" so that students didn't feel constrained and deprived of peer contact, and most importantly, letting every student know that the teacher expected them to learn because the teacher had the ability to teach them.

The need to control always comes from a sense of fear—fear of our own inadequacies or fear of the students that we are assigned to teach. Most fear of the students we teach comes from culturally conditioned beliefs; for example, they are undisciplined, aggressive, violent, out of control, and prone to riot, etc. There tends to be a long-standing, deep-seated historical fear of African Americans, especially males, in groups, whether it is on street corners, in school hallways, or classrooms. We rarely fear White, upper-class

Table 10.3. What, When, and Where to Refer

Incidents to Ignore

Habits (for example, sitting on legs,
    rocking in desk, chewing on pencil,
    shaking legs, tapping)
Noisy hair beads
Passing notes
Shirttail out
Pitching paper into trash
Chewing gum
Tapping another student
Nonverbal language: rolling eyes,
    popping lips

Incidents to Examine Classroom
Classroom Management Style
Excessive talking
Sleeping students
Tardies
Not bringing materials to class
Requests to go to bathroom
Students begin to converse after extended
    lecture (may need a break)
Sharpening pencil (inappropriate time)
Getting out of/remaining in desk
Name-calling
Picking on others

*Incidents Requiring Referral to Student
Support Team Administrator*
Fighting
Weapons
Threats
Defiant behavior
Sexual harassment

*Incidents to Take Advantage
of the Teachable Moment*
Name calling
Student says "I can't do this"
Ridiculing another child's clothing or work
Teasing other students
Tattling
Using inappropriate nonprofanity (for
    example, "frigging, sucks, crap, freaking")
Talking or laughing when another student
    is talking
Anger (count to ten)
Not wanting to play together

*Incidents Requiring a Referral
to a Counselor*
Bullying
Stealing
Fighting

To a Parent
Stealing
Bad language
Doesn't complete assignments
Fighting

To an Adult Mentor
Apathy (academics)
Doesn't complete assignments

To a Peer
Apathy (academics)
Behavior (better behaved student)
Academics (peer tutor)

males, even though this group of students has committed our greatest school tragedies.

Low expectations for behavior and fear are communicated nonverbally to students. They intuitively sense a teacher's fear and will test your resolve at every turn. They will also resent the fearful teacher because they are angered by the teacher's perception of them. The best rule to probably follow is to never teach a group of students that you fear. It is more productive for both you and the students if you teach those students with whom you are comfortable.

Dealing with fear issues and giving up the need to control African American students will be a great step toward decreasing tension in the classroom and improving relationships with African American students. This in no way implies that there should not be rules and expectations for appropriate behavior.

It is ironic that the best teachers are also the "toughest," in the sense that they have rules that they expect students to follow, not to control them but to make the classroom run more efficiently. They do not fear students and they feel no need to control students. Most importantly, they refuse to give their power away. These teachers trust their students to meet the high expectations they hold for them, they are always teaching in social as well as classroom situations, and they trust their power to teach and make a difference in the lives of all students with whom they come in contact.

COGNITIVE RESTRUCTURING PROCESS

As you read this section, it is important to remember that its intent is not teacher or administrator bashing; it is rather to enhance both personal and professional empowerment. Keep these three thoughts in mind: (1) "It is not my fault" (that I am the victim of a cultural conditioning process that promoted the learning of stereotypes), (2) "I can change" my knowledge base and belief system, and (3) "It is my ethical responsibility to change" (as a professional educator).

Cognitive restructuring is the modification, changing, or restructuring of one's beliefs. A belief is what we perceive to be true and is a learned cognitive pattern. When a belief is erroneous, it can be unlearned to produce a newer, more accurate, and effective cognitive pattern. As more accurate cognitions replace the faulty or erroneous ones, changes in behavior will occur. Therefore, as old beliefs based on myths and stereotypes are replaced by a new set of beliefs, more culturally responsible behaviors will be developed.

Awareness is the key to becoming more culturally responsible in our interactions with African American students. Ultimately, we must experience a CRI or Culturally Relevant Insight. A CRI results when some event occurs that enables or forces us to deal at the conscious level with some previously unconscious belief. Sometimes, we gain these insights through attending a workshop; at other times, we are forced to confront our beliefs when we work with or become friends with someone about whom we previously held stereotypical beliefs.

Hopefully, you will start to experience more CRIs after reading this book and completing the following four exercises. Because African Americans are most often involved in disciplinary referrals, the examples included in the awareness exercises are African American males.

Awareness Exercise #1

For each of the following stereotypes, list specific behaviors or actions that would indicate that you possibly hold beliefs about African American male students based on the stereotype. For example, if a teacher unconsciously believed that African American males were dishonest, he or she might automatically assume that when something in the classroom was missing, it was taken by an African American male. A teacher who held the beliefs that African American males were both intellectually inferior and dishonest might insist that an African American male student cheated when he made a good grade on a test.

STEREOTYPE BEHAVIOR/ACTION	TEACHER/ADMINISTRATOR BEHAVIOR/ACTION
Dishonest	
Aggressive/Violent	
Lazy	
Sexually Promiscuous	
Irresponsible	
Intellectually Inferior	
Dysfunctional Family	
Culturally Deprived	
Athletic	
Gang Member	

Ask yourself if, in any circumstances, you have demonstrated any of those behaviors or actions. Which of those behaviors or actions would, or have, students or parents felt that you demonstrated? If you are serious about this process, devise an anonymous method for your students to give you input regarding behaviors associated with each of the stereotypes. Finally, monitor your behaviors and actions. If the types of actions and behaviors you have listed occur, then spend some time reflecting on the possibly unconscious beliefs that you may hold about African American male students.

Awareness Exercise #2

Monitor your reactions to African American male students, especially when they are in groups, that is, walking down the corridor or sitting together in the cafeteria. When you feel a sense of fear, anger, or any discomfort, immediately ask yourself:

1. What am I thinking at this moment?

2. Is this thought related to a belief that I hold about African American males? What is the belief?
3. Is the belief connected to a myth or stereotype?
4. How does this thought influence my feelings and actions?

When time permits, again reflect on the thoughts and feelings you experienced. Ask yourself, "Can I honestly attribute the trait that made me feel uncomfortable to all African American male students? Why or why not? If all African American males are not the same, how can I change my beliefs and thoughts so that they are more objective and reflective of reality?" Practice identifying and refuting the erroneous beliefs when your feelings and actions indicate that they are operating at an unconscious level.

Awareness Exercise #3

Another activity that you can use to increase your ability to experience CRIs is to "replace the face." When you feel very annoyed, angered, or uncomfortable with the manner or actions of an African American male, visualize him with another face. Then ask yourself, "How would I respond if he were not African American? not male? not poor?" Monitor your reactions to the mannerisms and actions of students who are not African American males. In what ways do you react to these students differently? Why?

Awareness Exercise #4

According to Kuykendall (1992), several factors can influence the way that teachers perceive and react to students. These are a student's (1) name, (2) gender, (3) socioeconomic status, (4) previous academic record (and records of siblings), (5) previous conduct record (and records of siblings), and (6) appearance. Poor African American males are placed in triple jeopardy of being victims of negative perceptions, low expectations, and poor relationships with teachers.

It has been my experience, and shared with me by other African American teachers, that when a student has a name like Jerome or Jamal, a not-so-good academic record, a few previous conflicts with a teacher, and he is very tall and very dark in complexion, he is at a very real risk of receiving a disciplinary referral and subsequent punishment. Take some time to reflect on the characteristics or profiles that cause you the most difficulty in establishing rapport or communicating effectively with an African American male student.

These exercises are designed to help you engage in a process that will make it easier to identify, confront, and change erroneous beliefs so that you can demonstrate more culturally responsive and responsible behaviors toward African American students.

Parents can and should play a significant role in reducing disciplinary events and suspensions. In the next chapter, we discuss ways to involve parents and community members in the process.

RECOMMENDATIONS

Do: Complete the Cognitive Restructuring Exercises.

- If you feel comfortable in doing so, share your insights and feelings with a colleague.

Chapter 11

The Village Approach

Forming Partnerships with Parents and Community

In this book, I have primarily discussed the role and responsibility of the school in eliminating racial disparities in discipline. The research I have cited, my experiences as a race and gender consultant, and my discussions primarily with African American students, parents, teachers, administrators, and community members indicate that significant changes must be made in beliefs, attitudes, policies, and practices within the school setting if racial disparities in discipline are to be eliminated.

I often ask students how their parent(s) reacted to their suspension(s) and am amazed with their responses. They usually respond that the parent gets upset, maybe even angry, but when quizzed more about parental sanctions (i.e., grounding, withdrawal of privileges, etc.), there are usually none. We might infer two things from this apathetic behavior. One, we may believe that the parent just doesn't care about the child's misbehavior, or we may take this response as an indication of sense of powerlessness on the part of parents to impact school discipline policies.

One other possibility, however, is that the deep sense of distrust that now exists among African American parents toward the school may impact their response or lack of response. When asked how his parents responded to his out-of-school suspension, one African American male student told me his grandfather's response: "You got to watch some of those teachers; they try to get you in trouble, [they] don't want to see you go anywhere in life."

There is a very definite role that African American parents and community members must play in reducing disciplinary incidents and referrals among African American students. We need to ask the assistance of a core group of parents and community members in addressing the problem of disparity in discipline. It will be important to include adversaries as well as supporters, and individuals from all income strata.

A starting point might be to have parents and community members talk about their experiences in our schools, especially the way in which they experienced discipline policies and practices when they were students themselves. If these adults have had negative experiences in our schools because of cultural insensitivity, then we will necessarily have to start to build trust in our schools. Parents and community members must believe that their children will be treated fairly if they are to become our partners in resolving the problem.

FORMING A SCHOOL–COMMUNITY PARTNERSHIP

The first step in the process is to clarify the school's role and responsibility:

1. Ask for the assistance of the community in resolving the problem.
2. Acknowledge that there is a problem of racial disparity in discipline.
3. Acknowledge that the lack of cultural knowledge and unconscious stereotyping is a factor.
4. Make a commitment to take responsibility for changing the school climate.

Secondly, clarify the community's role and responsibility.

1. Express the expectation that the community will assist.
2. Try to involve ministers and express the desire that they take a leadership role in the process.
3. Express the expectation that knowledgeable community members will take a leadership role if it is difficult to recruit parents.
4. Expect ministers and community members to influence parents to be a part of the process.

Third, ask parents and community members to

1. Provide mentors for troubled students.
2. Serve on a task force to design discipline policies.
3. Serve on a task force to develop criteria for placement in alternative programs.
4. Serve as members of a support team for students with discipline problems.
5. Serve on committees to define disciplinary offenses.
6. Serve on hearing panels for serious offenses.

7. Conduct classes for students related to traditional African American beliefs and values.

Finally, conduct dialogues with parents and community members about

1. Their feelings related to race, racism, and bad experiences as a student.
2. Conflicts in parent and school values. For instance, fighting at school, even to defend oneself, is a punishable offense. Many African American parents, however, insist that their children "hit back" when hit. The child may even get into trouble at home for not defending himself. Many African American parents are authoritarian in their childrearing and believe in corporal punishment, that is, spanking or "whipping." Some African American parents feel that their rights as a parent to discipline their children in a way that they feel is best have been taken away.
3. Provide information to
   a. Parents and community members about the process for filing complaints or grievances.
   b. Teachers and administrators about African American culture and the issues that African American males face.
4. Provide support to
   a. Single mothers and grandmothers raising children alone.
   b. Community groups who are willing to sponsor community-run programs for students with serious behavior problems. The strategies will be helpful in forming a partnership with parents and the community that will help increase communication, build trust, and provide a cooperative effort to decrease discipline problems.

We have examined data, school-related factors related to disparity in discipline, i.e., cultural conflict and stereotypes, and school climate. We have discussed the role that administrators, individual teachers, parents, and community can play in the process of reducing disciplinary events and suspensions. Finally, in the next chapter, we evaluate the process.

RECOMMENDATIONS

Do: Begin a dialogue with parents about their school experiences.

• Initiate a partnership with parents and community members to address issues related to the school climate and discipline.

Chapter 12

Evaluating the Process

School Climate and Individual Assessment

How do you know that the process you have undertaken to eliminate school-related factors that place African American male students at risk for disciplinary referrals and action is working? The most effective test is that you will see a decrease in the number of disciplinary referrals for African American students; if you are in a predominately African American school setting, you will see a decrease in disciplinary referrals in general. A by-product of this process can also be that you will have fewer complaints voiced and filed by African American parents.

Creating an environment that is characterized by culturally responsive and culturally responsible behaviors is an ongoing process that will not only produce significant differences in the area of discipline but will influence the total school environment.

Evaluating the effectiveness of the change process involves conducting assessments at both the school climate and individual level. The first set of questions below involves an assessment of the school climate. The questions that follow relate not only to the disciplinary process but also to all aspects of the school culture. The questions will refer to "African American students"; if your school has a majority African American student population, rephrase the question to read, "African American students from lower socioeconomic backgrounds."

SCHOOL CLIMATE ASSESMENT

Answer "yes" or "no" to each item. If you answer "yes" to an item, give specific examples to support your response.

1. Are high expectations (academic performance and social behavior) held for African American students?
2. Do African American students feel respected and accepted in the school environment?
3. Do African American students feel a sense of connectedness to the school community?
4. Is the language and culture of African American students respected and valued?
5. Are African American students free to express their cultural identity?
6. Do the formal and informal curricula include the accomplishments and contributions of Africans and African Americans?
7. Is creating a culturally sensitive and responsive school environment a school goal?
8. Is reducing the number of disciplinary referrals involving African American students, especially males, a priority issue?
9. Are disciplinary referrals for African American students, especially African American males, proportionate to their numbers in the school population?
10. Has a diverse committee (race, ethnicity, social class, teachers, students, parents, community members) been established to periodically review discipline policies and issues?
11. Have discipline policies and procedures been established that eliminate disparity related to race, gender, and social class?
12. Is disaggregated data (race, gender, social class) related to academic performance and discipline reviewed periodically?
13. Do instructional and resource materials have African American representation?
14. Does a representative number of African American students participate in all types of extracurricular activities?
15. Does a representative number of African American students hold leadership positions in student government and organizations?
16. Are African American students represented in all academic levels, for example, gifted, honors, etc., in proportion to their numbers in the school population?
17. Do teaching styles and assessment procedures reflect an understanding of the culture and experiences of African American students?
18. Do African American parents feel comfortable and welcome in the school environment?
19. Is the faculty comfortable interacting with African American parents?
20. Is the school's stated emphasis one of academic achievement rather than discipline and control?

21. Does discipline focus on teaching appropriate behavior as well as punishment?
22. Are all allegations of racism, sexism, and classism investigated?
23. Is ongoing professional development and technical assistance provided for faculty and staff related to cultural differences, stereotyping, discipline, etc.?
24. Is coaching provided for faculty members who have persistent problems with African American students?
25. Is coaching provided for faculty members who are resistant to the process of becoming more culturally responsive and responsible?
26. Is coaching provided for faculty members who receive a disproportionate number of persistent complaints from students and parents?
27. Are there sanctions against negative "lounge talk" about students?
28. Are culturally responsive and responsible behaviors included in the criteria for faculty evaluations and accountability?
29. Is hiring more African American and other faculty members of color a priority?
30. Is the climate assessment an ongoing process?

INDIVIDUAL ASSESSMENT

An assessment at the individual level will help teachers and administrators to know how they are progressing in terms of the process of becoming more culturally responsive and responsible. As was the case with the assessment of the school climate, affirmative responses given for the questions asked will indicate that the teacher or administrator has developed the beliefs and is demonstrating behaviors that make all students feel respected and valued.

Answer "yes" or "no" to each item. If you answer "yes" to an item, give specific examples to support your response.

1. Do I see the need to focus on the issues of groups of students who are experiencing difficulties, that is, African American males?
2. Am I open to participating in the process to develop more culturally responsive and responsible behaviors?
3. Am I willing to learn more about the culture of African American students?
4. Do I practice cultural etiquette as it relates to African American students?
5. Am I comfortable discussing issues related to race, culture, and social class?
6. Am I comfortable dealing with issues related to race, culture, and social class?

7. Am I effective in dealing with issues related to race, culture, and social class?

8. Do I monitor my own behavior to be sure that I am not reacting on the basis on unconscious stereotyping?

9. Do I work to establish rapport and build effective relationships with African American students?

10. Have I set a goal for reducing disciplinary referrals involving African American male students?

11. Do I understand my own power issues and find "win–win" ways to gain the respect of students?

12. Have I overcome my fear of African American males?

13. Do I seek the advice of other colleagues when I am experiencing difficulty with a particular student?

14. Do I seek to understand the motivation for student misbehavior?

15. When I have persistent conflict with a student, do I
    a. seek to dialogue with the student?
    b. examine my own beliefs and behaviors?
    c. take seriously any comment made by the student about feeling that he is the victim of racism, prejudice, etc., and seek to discover why he feels this way?

16. Do I allow students who have misbehaved to "start anew"?

17. Do I seek input from students regarding classroom rules and issues related to discipline?

18. Do I, to the best of my ability, try to see the world through the "eyes of my students"?

19. Have I made a commitment to be more effective in relating to and communicating with African American males?

20. Do I handle "non-serious" disciplinary issues in my classroom?

21. Do I examine the "precipitating factors" when an incident occurs?

22. Am I aware of my beliefs and behaviors that cause an incident to escalate?

23. Am I aware of my beliefs and behaviors that facilitate establishing good relationships with African American male students?

24. Am I aware of my beliefs and behaviors that hinder my establishing good relationships with African American male students?

25. Do I "see and respect" color (differences)?

26. Do I seek to dialogue with parents about student misbehavior before it reaches a serious level?

27. Am I willing to engage in conflict resolution with a student?

28. Do I always conduct myself in a professional and ethical manner with students?

29. Do I take advantage of "teachable moments" to help students understand why certain behavior is inappropriate?
30. Do I engage in an ongoing process of reflection and self-assessment?

The climate and individual assessments were designed to serve as an indicator of the extent to which new belief systems and modes of behavior are being instituted in the school environment. They provide a measure of the type of changes that individual teachers and administrators are making as well as the impact these changes have on the total school culture.

CONCLUSION

Culturally responsible actions are those that ensure students will not receive disparate treatment as a result of conscious or unconscious bias or prejudices. In this instance, culturally responsible actions are those taken to prevent African American students from being the victims of historical myths and stereotypes. This change is based on the recognition that stereotypical images of African American males, in particular, are both persistent and pervasive. They are also perpetuated through a cultural conditioning process from which teachers are not immune.

Stereotyping is a sensitive issue that many teachers and administrators find very difficult to acknowledge and talk about. The mere mention of the word "stereotype" often brings about immediate denials, defensiveness, and the "I am the exception syndrome," where individuals seek to prove that they remained untouched by the cultural conditioning process.

At the institutional or school climate level, changes that relate to cultural responsiveness involve professional development and modifications in school practices so that students are not penalized for cultural differences. Changes related to cultural responsibility include a system of teacher accountability and evaluation that emphasizes the teacher's ability to demonstrate culturally sensitive and responsive behaviors toward all students.

At the individual level, cultural responsiveness involves the practice of cultural etiquette or social forms that respect the preferences and taboos of cultural groups. Changes related to cultural responsibility will involve cognitive restructuring, a process of modifying beliefs that are based on historical myths and stereotypes.

It is imperative that we give our attention to what is happening to African American students. The disciplinary process as it is currently implemented has almost predictable outcomes, all of which are negative and especially place young African American males at risk for negative consequences in the larger society. Research (Mendez, 2003; Mendez and Knoff, 2003) and my own practical experience in talking to and working with students tells us is that exclusionary discipline does not work. We know that

- Suspension does not decrease inappropriate behavior; students that I interviewed reported that being suspended did nothing to change their behavior; when they felt they were unfairly suspended, it only increased their anger and potential for "defiant" behavior.
- Suspension is not a deterrent to either suspended or non-suspended students; daily students see other students suspended and participate in the same types of behavior.
- Suspension is pervasive. For African American males, suspension begins in elementary school and continues through high school; when asked about "the first time you remember getting into trouble," most responded that the first incident for which they were suspended occurred in elementary or middle school.
- Suspension leads to repeated suspensions; over 50% of students I interviewed had been suspended repeatedly.
- Suspension is negatively related to academic achievement; students interviewed reported falling behind in classes after the first 3–5 day suspension and getting failing grades with each subsequent suspension.

Perhaps it is time that we examine the issues again and try some new approaches. I offer this book as another way to view the problem. Character education and other behavioral change programs for students have been found to decrease school suspensions, but they do not address the core issues that are the root causes of disciplinary events in the classroom.

So, where does that leave us as educators? First, we must acknowledge that culture and group membership to a very large extent determines who gets referred for disciplinary actions. Second, we must recognize that exclusionary discipline works against all of our best intentions to adequately educate those most at-risk for non-completion. Finally, we must do all within our power to examine and change those things within the school setting itself which contribute to disparity in discipline.

We have spent more money and time imaginable trying to "fix students" and their parents while ignoring some core social problems in this society that affect our schools, just as they do every other institution in America. It is time to honestly face ourselves, to make some fundamental changes, and to make our schools places of emotional, as well as physical, safety. No student should be the victim of the harm that results from ignorance of his culture or the stigma imposed by historical images.

RECOMMENDATIONS

Do: Continue the process that has begun.

• Make maintaining equity in school discipline a priority.

Afterword

Why should we believe that significant racial and ethnic disparities in educational outcomes could ever go away without frank and thoughtful discussion? You have in your hands a guide to opening that discussion, a blueprint for asking questions that need to be asked to confront the complex issues of educational inequity.

Educators are, by nature and training, truly excellent problem-solvers. Given the recognition of a problem, and the opportunity to address it, teachers, administrators, and support staff rarely fail to develop the solutions that can improve their students' educational outcomes.

With the courage to recognize and reflect upon disparities in their own school, and with resources like *Cultures In Conflict,* there is no question in my mind that America's educators can effectively bring those problem-solving skills to bear on issues of educational inequity.

Russell J. Skiba, Ph.D.
Professor, Counseling and Educational Psychology
Center for Evaluation and Educational Policy
Indiana University
Bloomington, Indiana

Appendix

The African American Male School Experience

An item that I often include on a beliefs survey when I conduct workshops with teachers and administrators is this : All students, regardless of racial, cultural, or social class background have the same in-school learning opportunities.

I always emphasize the "in-school" experience, and ask the participants not to think of anything but what happens to the student after he sets foot on the school grounds. Initially, many participants will agree that all students have the same and equal opportunities to learn in the school setting. Some even suggest that since minority and poor students often attend schools or participate in programs that receive large amounts of federal aid, they actually have greater learning opportunities than other students.

After some discussion and reflection, however, there is usually agreement that all students do not have the same learning opportunities in the school setting. Students have the same status and experiences in our schools as they have in the larger society, of which the school is a microcosm. Students who belong to stigmatized groups in the larger society belong to stigmatized groups in our schools. African American males are a stigmatized group within the larger American society, and African American male students belong to a stigmatized group in most school settings.

The moment of greatest opportunity for any student is when he or she is interacting with his or her teacher. Students who belong to stigmatized groups do not have the same interactions with their teachers as their more privileged peers. When a student is feared, believed to be of poor moral character, or believed to be intellectually inferior, it is difficult for him to have interactions that provide him with the fullest opportunity to excel as a student.

What is it like to be an African American male student? Given the lack of understanding of his culture, the disdain for his mannerisms, and the misperceptions about him, it is not likely to be a very pleasant experience. Often, he does not understand why he is disliked or feared, or why so little is expected and thought of him. He feels powerless to change any of the feelings and opinions that are held of him. He only knows that he must constantly be on guard.

When I inquired of African American male teachers what it is like to be the victim of myths and stereotypes, they had some very strong and definite feelings. There comments are summarized below.

"It hurts."

"It's sad."

"No matter what you do, nothing changes."

"I'm tired of proving myself."

"You hold it in."

"It's not fair."

"I'm always prepared to challenge."

"I'm not a bad person."

"I get angry."

The response heard most often from the group was that they became angry. Anger, in fact, is the most common human response to a sense of powerlessness. We encounter very angry African American male students each day; some of the anger stems from their view of their place in the world, some is their response to bad home situations, and some comes from the sense of frustration and powerlessness that they feel in the school setting.

This anger is turned either inward or outward. When the anger is turned inward, we find African American male students who are depressed, who suffer from psychosomatic ills, who abuse alcohol and drugs, who engage in reckless and self-destructive behaviors, and some who—in increasing numbers—commit suicide.

When young African American males direct the anger outward (which is a common human behavior resulting from the sense of powerlessness), they engage in aggressive and violent behavior. Much of the aggressive behavior that we see directed toward teachers comes from this sense of powerlessness. Many conflicts between African American males and teachers result from power struggles or the student's perception of the abuse of power.

Stereotyping, conscious or unconscious, produces a sense of powerlessness in the African American male, and subsequently leads to conflict. Creating a school culture, in which the culture of the African American male is respected and where stereotyping is not tolerated, will help to decrease both the anger and the aggressive behavior so often seen in young African American males.

Bibliography

Advancement Project and Civil Rights Project. 2000. Opportunities Suspended: The Devastating Consequences of Zero Tolerance and School Discipline. Washington, DC: Advancement Project; Cambridge, MA: Harvard University, Civil Rights Project.

Althen, G. 1988. American Ways: A Guide for Foreigners in the United States. Yarmouth, ME: Intercultural Press.

Applied Research Center. 2000. Facing the Consequences: An Examination of Racial Discrimination in U.S. Public Schools. ERASE Report. Oakland, CA: Applied Research Center, ERASE Initiative.

Atkinson, D., G. Morten, and D. Sue, eds. 1983. Counseling American Minorities: A Cross-cultural Perspective, 2nd ed. Dubuque, IA: William C. Brown.

Bireda, M. 2000. The Mythical African American Male, WEEA Digest. Newton, MA: WEEA Resource Center.

Boskin, J. 1970. The National Jester in the Popular Culture. In The Great Fear, pp. 165–85, Gary Nash and Richard Weiss, eds. New York: Holt, Rinehart, and Winston

———. 1986. The Rise and Demise of an American Jester. New York: Oxford University Press.

Brown, J.A., D. J. Losen, and J. Wald. 2001. Zero Tolerance: Unfair With Little Recourse. In New Directions For Youth Development, Zero Tolerance: Can Suspension and Expulsion Keep Schools Safe?, pp. 73–100, R. J. Skiba and G. G. Noam, eds. San Franciso: Jossey Bass.

Butler, J. P. 1992. Of Kindred Minds: The Ties That Bind. In Cultural Competence for Educators, pp. 23–54, Mario A. Orlandi, ed. Rockville, MD: U.S. Department of Health and Human Services.

Children's Defense Fund. Children Out of School in America. Washington, DC: Children's Defense Fund of the Washington Research Report.

Dandy, E. B. 1991. *Black Communication: Breaking Down the Barriers*. Chicago: African American Images.

Eyler, J., V. Cook, and L. Ward. 1983. Resegregation: Segregation within Desegregated Schools. In *The Consequences of School Desegregation*, Christine Rossell and Willis D. Hawley, eds. Philadelphia, PA: Temple University Press.

Glasser, William. 1986. *Control Theory in the Classroom*. New York: Harper Row.

Greenfield, P. M., C. Raeff, and B. Quiroz. 1996. Cultural Values in Learning and Education. In *Closing the Achievement Gap: A Vision for Changing Beliefs and Practices*, pp. 37–55, Belinda Ho, ed. Arlington, VA: Association for Supervision and Curriculum Development.

Hale-Benson, J. E. 1986. *Black Children: Their Roots, Culture, and Learning Styles*. Baltimore, MD: John Hopkins University Press.

Herskovits, M. J. 1958. *The Myth of the Negro Past*. Boston: Beacon Press.

Hillard, A. 1986. Alternatives to IQ Testing: An Approach to the Identification of Gifted Minority Children. In *Black Children: Their Roots, Culture, and Learning Styles*, p. 43, J. E. Benson, ed. Baltimore, MD: John Hopkins University Press.

Ho, M. K. 1987. *Family Therapy with Ethnic Minorities*. Newbury, CA: Sage.

Hodgkinson, H. 2000. *Secondary Schools in a New Millennium: Demographic Certainties, Social Realities*. Reston, VA: National Association of Secondary School Principals.

Hyman, I. A., and P. A. Snook. 1999. *Dangerous Schools: What We Can Do about the Physical and Emotional Abuse of Our Children*. San Francisco: Jossey-Bass Publishers.

Johnston, R. 2000. *Education News* June 21. Federal Data Highlight Disparities in Discipline.

Joint Center for Political Studies. 1989. Visions of a Better Way: A Black Appraisal of Public Schooling. Washington, DC: Joint Center for Political Studies Press.

Kuykendall, C. 1992. *From Rage to Hope: Strategies for Reclaiming Black and Hispanic Students*. Bloomington, IN: National Educational Service.

Locke, D. C. 1992. *Increasing Multicultural Understanding: A Comprehensive Model*. Newbury Park, CA: Sage.

Loewenberg, P. 1970. The Psychology of Racism. In *The Great Fear*, Gary Nash and Richard Weiss, eds. New York: Holt, Rinehart, & Winston.

Lynch, E. W., and M. J. Hanson. 1992. *Developing Cross-cultural Competence: A Guide for Working with Young Children and Their Families*. Baltimore, MD: Paul H. Brookes Publishing.

Mattison, E., and M. S. Abner. 2007. Closing The Achievement Gap: The Association of Racial Climate with Achievement and Behavioral Outcomes. *American Journal of Community Psychology*, Vol. 40.

Mendez, L. M. R. 2003. Predictors of suspension and Negative School Outcomes: A Longitudinal Investigation. In *New Directions For Youth Development, no. 99, Deconstructing The School To-Prison Pipeline*, pp. 17–33. J. Wald and D. J. Losen, eds. San Franciso: Jossey Bass.

Mendez, L. M. R., and H. M. Knoff. 2003. Who Gets Suspended From School and Why? A Demographic Analysis of Schools and Disciplinary Infractions In A Large School District. *Education and Treatment of Children*, Vol. 26, No. 1.

Meirer, K., J. Stewart, and R. England. 1989. *Race, Class, and Education: The Politics of Second-Generation Discrimination.* Madison: University of Wisconsin Press.

Newby, I. A. 1965. *Jim Crow's Defense: Anti-Negro Thought in America 1900–1930.* Baton Rouge: Louisiana State University.

Office of Civil Rights. 1974. Student Discipline. Washington, DC: HEW Fact Sheet.

———. 1994. Racial Incidents and Harassment against Students at Educational Institutional Guidance, no. 59. Washington, DC: Federal Register 11448, March 10.

———. 2001. Proactive Docket Activities—Fiscal Year 2001. Atlanta, GA: Southern Division.

———. 2001–2002. Annual Report to Congress. Part 3, Strategic Priorities. Retrieved on 6/17/09 from: http:/www.ed.gov/about/offices/list/ocr/AnnRpt2002/edlite-2002arc-3html.

Ogbu, J. 1978. *Minority Education and Caste: The American System in Cross-cultural Perspective.* New York: Academic Press.

Oliver, W. 1998. Reflections on Manhood. In *Images of Color: Images of Crime,* p. 81, Coramae Mann and Marjorie Zatz, eds. Los Angeles: Roxbury.

Paul, A. M. 1998. Where Bias Begins: The Truth about Stereotypes, *Psychology Today* 31 (May/June): 52–56.

Peretti, P. O. 1983. Effects of Teacher's Attitudes on Discipline Problems in Schools Recently Desegregated. In *The Consequences of School Desegregation,* Christine Rossell and Willis Hawley, eds. Philadelphia: Temple University Press.

Rausch, M. K. and R. J. Skiba. The Academic Cost of Discipline: The Relationship Between Suspensdion/Expulsion and School Achievement. Retrieved 2/5/09 from: http://www.agi.harvard.edu/Search/download.php?id=45.

Reddick, L. D. 1944. The Nineteen Basic Stereotypes of Blacks in American Society. *Journal of Negro Education* 12.

Rome, D. 1998. Stereotyping by the Media: Murderers, Rapists, and Drug Addicts. in *Images of Color: Images of Crime,* pp. 86–87, Coramae Mann and Marjorie Zatz, eds., Los Angeles: Roxbury.

Skiba, R. J., and K. Knesting. 2001. Zero Tolerance, Zero Evidence: An Analysis of School Disciplinary Practice. In *New Directions For Youth Development, Zero Tolerance: Can Suspension and Expulsion Keep Schools Safe?,* pp. 17–44, R. J. Skiba and G. G. Noam, eds. San Francisco: Jossey Bass.

Skiba, R. J., R. S. Michael, A. C. Nardo, and R. Peterson. 2002. The color of discipline: Sources of racial and gender disproportionality in school punishment. *The Urban Review,* 34, 317–342.

Sobel, M. 1987. *The World They Made Together: Black and White Values in Eighteenth-Century Virginia.* Princeton, NJ: Princeton University Press.

Wallace, J. M., S. Goodkind, C. M. Wallace, and J. G. Bachman. 2008. Racial, Ethnic, and Gender Differences. In School Discipline Among U.S. High School Students: 1991–2005. *Negro Educational Review*, 59 1–2, 47–62.

Wald, J., and D. Losen. 2003. Defining And Redirecting A School-to-Prison Pipeline. In *New Directions For Youth Development, no. 99, Deconstructing The School-To- Prison Pipeline,* pp. 9–15, J. Wald and D. J. Losen, eds. San Francisco: Jossey-Bass.

Willis, W. 1992. Families with African American Roots. In *Developing Cross-Cultural Competence: A Guide for Working with Young Children and Their Families*, E. W. Lynch and M. J. Hanson, eds. Baltimore, MD: Paul H. Brookes.

Witt, H. 2007. School Discipline Harder on Blacks: Analysis of Federal Data Shows Racial Inequity in Suspensions and Expulsions Nationwide; Locally the Gap is Widest in Lake and Dupage. Retrieved 6/18/09 from http:/archives.chicagotribune.com/2007/sep/25/news/discipline

Wynn, C. 1983. Black and White Bibb County Classrooms. In *The Consequences of School Desegregation,* p. 145, Christine Rossell and Willis Hawley, eds. Philadelphia: Temple University Press.

Zuniga, M. 1992. Families with Latino Roots. In *Developing Cross-cultural Competence: A Guide for Working with Young Children and Their Families*, E. W. Lynch and M. J. Hanson, eds. Baltimore, MD: Paul H. Brookes.

About the Author

Martha R. Bireda has been an educational consultant for twenty years, specializing in racial disparity in discipline and the racial achievement gap. She received her Ed.S. and Ph.D. in Counselor Education from the University of Florida in Gainesville.